PERSON
OF
INTEREST

INVESTIGATOR'S GUIDE

PERSON OF INTEREST

INVESTIGATOR'S GUIDE

WHY JESUS STILL MATTERS IN A WORLD THAT REJECTS THE BIBLE

10 SESSIONS

J. WARNER WALLACE

ZONDERVAN
REFLECTIVE

ZONDERVAN REFLECTIVE

Person of Interest Investigator's Guide
Copyright © 2021 by J. Warner Wallace

Requests for information should be addressed to:
Zondervan, *3900 Sparks Dr. SE, Grand Rapids, Michigan 49546*

Zondervan titles may be purchased in bulk for educational, business, fundraising, or sales promotional use. For information, please email SpecialMarkets@Zondervan.com.

ISBN 978-0-310-11134-4 (softcover)

ISBN 978-0-310-11135-1 (ebook)

Published in association with the literary agency of Mark Sweeney & Associates, Chicago, Illinois 60611.

Cover Design: Darren Welch
Cover Images: © Eakachai Leesin / Shutterstock; © Undrey / Shutterstock
Interior Design: J. Warner Wallace
Interior Illustrations: Copyright © 2021 by J. Warner Wallace
Interior Typesetting: Kait Lamphere
Fingerprint image: © Musa Studio / Shutterstock
Shoeprint image: © Lucky Strokes / Shutterstock

Printed in the United States of America

HB 04.11.2024

CONTENTS

CONTENTS

A NOTE FROM J. WARNER

Welcome to the *Person of Interest Investigator's Guide*. This casebook, created to be used with its accompanying video sessions, was written as a supplement to my book *Person of Interest*. I believe this investigation is more important now than ever before. Confidence in the teaching of the New Testament is lower than in prior generations; the youngest among us are more uninterested than any other age group. Many skeptics deny the reliability of the New Testament gospels, and even *believers* are skeptical or uninformed about what the Bible teaches on the deity of Christ. For many, Jesus has become a misunderstood, irrelevant relic from the past.

Did Jesus really live? Can we reconstruct the truth about Jesus even if we *don't* trust the New Testament? Are there any good reasons to believe he existed or that he was anything other than an ancient sage? Why should I care about Jesus? Does he still matter *today*? Is Jesus truly history's most important "person of interest," and if so, how does this conclusion affect me? That's what this investigation is all about.

To get the most out of this study, I hope you dig deeper into the evidence you are about to examine by reviewing my complete investigation in the book *Person of Interest*. We will only scratch the surface here, and Jesus is too important to treat lightly. If Jesus of Nazareth is who he claimed, this investigation will be more important than anything you've ever studied. The more you learn about the evidence for Jesus (and the incomparable impact he's had on human history), the better you'll be able to assess his role in *your* life and make the case to others.

I was a thirty-five-year-old committed atheist when I first began to sift through the evidence related to Jesus. I was also a successful detective in Los Angeles County. In this investigative series, I will tell you why I first became interested in Jesus and how I employed a unique fact-finding template to discover the truth about him. I will also describe one of my cases and show you how the approach I used to solve that case helped me to uncover the truth about Jesus. I've changed several names and swapped details of my criminal cases to protect the identity of victims (and suspects) and to safeguard the progress of cases still under investigation.

When our investigation is complete, you'll understand why I'm a Christian today, and you'll also understand why Jesus *matters*, even if you're skeptical about the New Testament gospels.

J. Warner Wallace, *Dateline*-featured cold-case detective, and author of *Person of Interest*

HOW TO USE THIS GUIDE

The *Person of Interest Investigator's Guide* is designed to be experienced in a group setting (a Bible study, Sunday school class, or small group gathering). Each session begins with a "Case Briefing" section, opening questions to get you thinking about the investigation, and a "Statement Analysis" section to discuss the Bible passages. I will then guide you through the investigation in the video. Afterward, you'll work together as an investigative team to examine the evidence and engage in a follow-up investigation. Each session ends with a chance to debrief, deliberate, and pray.

To make the most out of this investigation, each member should have his or her own copy of this investigative guide and a Bible. Don't worry about which Scripture translation you use; you'll be able to glean the evidence from whatever version you're accustomed to. You'll be encouraged to examine *all* the evidence by reading the relevant content in *Person of Interest*, which chronicles the investigation more thoroughly and provides deeper insight into the case for Jesus and his impact on history. It is best to read the book *alongside* this investigative guide, and I will provide you with direction each week in the "Making the Case" section.

Please note: This is no ordinary "Bible study." Each investigative session is longer than a typical small group session. If you decide to complete each session in its entirety, please give yourself one to two hours to watch the video and work through the group investigation together.

To get the most out of this series, remember the following:

1. Investigative teams (especially homicide detectives) make the most progress when they are *interactive*. For this reason, you'll make the greatest headway (and experience the most spiritual growth) during your *small group interactions*. Think about the investigation as you experience it, discuss with one another what you've discovered, ask questions, and learn from one another as you share what God has revealed to you. You can't be a part of an investigative team if you aren't present, so do your best to attend each session. *Committed* investigators are *successful* investigators.

2. I've been a member of many investigative teams. The most successful were those where each of us, as detectives, respected and trusted one another enough to share our theories, intuitions, and hunches confidentially (without the fear of being mocked or embarrassed). In a similar way, your small group will experience the most from this investigation if it is a place where people can share safely, learn about Jesus, and build intimacy, friendship, and trust with confidentiality. Do your best to make your group a secure place to explore and share the truth. Be honest with one another, and listen compassionately to each other's private observations and opinions.

I learned early on that investigations are seldom limited to a nine-to-five workday. Some of my best thinking occurred after hours. That's why I want to encourage you to conduct the secondary investigations I've provided between the sessions. You can conduct these investigations in a single sitting or stretch them out over the course of the week. But even if you're unable to complete the secondary investigations, don't let that inhibit your attendance for the following week. You'll still be a valuable contributor, even if you haven't "done your homework." You don't want to miss the opportunity to experience Jesus as a person of interest.

Note: If you are a lead investigator (a group leader), check out the additional instructions and resources in the back of this investigative guide.

THE FUSE AND THE FALLOUT

Truth will come to sight; murder cannot be hid long.

—WILLIAM SHAKESPEARE

📁 CASE BRIEFING

Do you know anyone who is skeptical of the New Testament? Have *you* ever doubted the accuracy of the Gospels? In this opening investigation, we'll examine a detective technique you can use to examine the historicity and deity of Jesus from an unusual perspective: *without any evidence from the New Testament.*

You read that correctly.

When I investigated the existence and deity of Jesus, I quickly realized the Bible wasn't the only available source of information. I didn't need the evidence provided by the New Testament gospels to know the truth about Jesus. In fact, if some evil regime had destroyed every existing Christian Bible before I was born—if there hadn't been a single biblical New Testament manuscript to testify about the life or deity of Jesus—I would *still* have been able to determine the truth about him.

How? By investigating the case for Jesus like a "no-body homicide" cold case.

In this opening session, I'll describe the simple investigative strategy I've used to solve no-body homicide cases, which we can also apply to the case for Jesus. If you're someone who rejects the New Testament, as I did, you may be shocked at how much you can still learn about Jesus, even *without* relying on the Bible for information.

When your investigation is complete, you'll determine if Jesus *matters*. You'll discover if he was a work of fiction, just another ancient sage, or history's uniquely divine person of interest.

When detectives gather to "brief" before a long investigation, they usually have the advantage of being familiar with one another. That may not be the case for your group. Take a few minutes to introduce yourselves. Then, to start off the investigation on the right foot, briefly engage one of the following topics:

- Share one hope or expectation you have for this examination of Jesus as a person of interest.
  —or—
- Share why you think some people are skeptical about the existence or deity of Jesus.

OPENING CLUES

Before watching the video, invite someone to read aloud the following passage from the gospel of Mark. Listen carefully to the way Jesus is described:

> Now after John was taken into custody, Jesus came into Galilee, preaching the gospel of God, and saying, "The time is fulfilled, and the kingdom of God is at hand; repent and believe in the gospel."
>
> As He was going along the Sea of Galilee, He saw Simon and Andrew, the brother of Simon, casting a net in the sea; for they were fishermen. And Jesus said to them, "Follow Me, and I will have you become fishers of people." Immediately they left their nets and followed Him. And going on a little farther, He saw James the son of Zebedee, and his brother John, who were also in the boat mending the nets. Immediately He called them; and they left their father Zebedee in the boat with the hired men, and went away to follow Him.
>
> They went into Capernaum; and immediately on the Sabbath Jesus entered the synagogue and began to teach. And they were amazed at His teaching; for He was teaching them as one having authority, and not as the scribes. (Mark 1:14–22)

Now ask someone to read this passage from Paul's letter to the Colossians:

> I want you to know how great a struggle I have in your behalf and for those who are at Laodicea, and for all those who have not personally seen my face, that their hearts may be encouraged, having been knit together in love, and that they would

attain to all the wealth that comes from the full assurance of understanding, resulting in a true knowledge of God's mystery, that is, Christ Himself, in whom are hidden all the treasures of wisdom and knowledge. (Colossians 2:1–3)

STATEMENT ANALYSIS

Spend a few minutes reflecting on the verses you just read, then discuss these questions with your group:

From what you read in Mark's gospel, what is different about the teaching of Jesus? What separated him from others teaching at the time? What do you think he said that impressed his listeners?

From Paul's letter to the Colossians, why is the teaching of Jesus unique? How would you rate the intelligence of Jesus compared with that of others, and on what are you basing your rating?

SURVEILLANCE VIDEO

Play the video for session 1. As you watch, use the following section of your investigator's guide to record any thoughts or concepts that stand out to you.

Notes related to Tammy Hayes's no-body homicide case:

_____

_____

_____

_____

Notes related to J. Warner's experience in church:

_____

_____

_____

_____

_____

NO-BODY HOMICIDES

No-body homicide cases are incredibly difficult to investigate and prosecute. Few of these cases are ever filed with the district attorney because prosecutors must (1) prove the victim was murdered (and isn't simply missing) and (2) prove that the defendant committed the crime. These types of murders require a special approach to solve and communicate to a jury. This unique approach can also be used to investigate the case for Jesus.

Notes related to the pastor's claim about Jesus:

_____

_____

_____

Notes related to the *fuse* and *fallout* technique:

_____

_____

_____

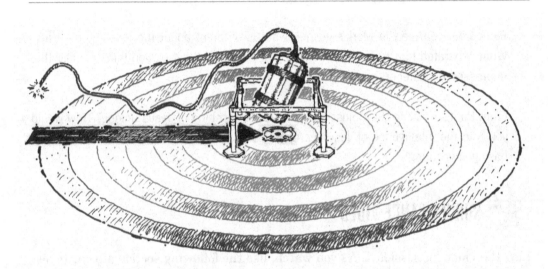

The FUSE and the FALLOUT will identify the FELON

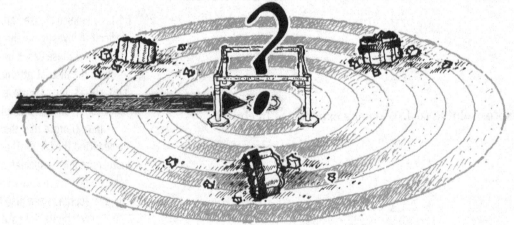

FOLLOW-UP INVESTIGATION

Now that you've watched the video as a group, engage the following questions and discuss what you've just examined with other members of your investigative team:

(1) Why are people interested in wisdom, even if it comes from an ancient source?

_____

_____

_____

(2) What is valuable about the *fuse* and *fallout* approach to solving mysteries?

_____

_____

_____

(3) **Read Luke 2:41–52.** Jesus's wisdom impressed his listeners, even when he was a young boy. What kinds of questions do you imagine Jesus was asking of the teachers in the temple? What is the importance of Jesus's statement to his parents about being in his father's house? What is the connection between Jesus's identity and his wisdom? Why is the deity of Jesus important to a world that is trying to decide why Jesus still matters?

_____

_____

_____

(4) **Read Matthew 13:53–58.** Once again Jesus's wisdom is recognized, even early in his ministry. Why is it sometimes hard for those who know us best to accept our advice, knowledge, or wisdom? Why are some people today hesitant to embrace the teaching of Jesus?

_____

_____

_____

Read 1 Corinthians 1:18–25. In this passage, one form of wisdom is compared with another. In the last two verses, why is the deity of Christ essential to the notion that he is uniquely wise and worthy of our attention?

_____

_____

_____

_____

 Consider the *fuse* and *fallout* model described in the video (see pages 4 and 5). Which aspects of ancient history (from the fuse, prior to 1 CE) would you expect to prepare for, anticipate, or predict the arrival of Jesus?

_____

_____

_____

_____

Which aspects of modern history (from the fallout, after 1 CE) would you expect to reflect Jesus's influence?

_____

_____

_____

_____

 ## DEBRIEF, DELIBERATE, AND PRAY

Pray as a team before you close your time together. Ask God to prepare you to rethink your notions of Jesus. Ask him to prepare others in your life to hear what you are going to learn in this investigation. Identify the prayer requests of others on your team so you can pray for them this week:

_____

_____

_____

_____

_____

Session 1

SECONDARY INVESTIGATION

 ## SUMMARIZING THE EVIDENCE

Before you begin this secondary investigation, briefly review your surveillance video notes from session 1. In the space below, write the most significant point(s) you took away from this session.

_____

_____

_____

 ## CONDUCTING A FORENSIC INVESTIGATION
Collecting the Evidence from Scripture

Collect the Evidence: Read Matthew 22:37–38; 1 Thessalonians 5:19–21; 1 John 4:1; Romans 14:5; and 2 Timothy 3:14.

Examine the Facts: Jesus tells us (in the passage from the gospel of Matthew) that we are to love God with our minds as well as our hearts and souls. God wants us to examine all the evidence at our disposal and to study the things of God with great intensity. When we do this, we truly begin to worship him with our minds, as described in today's other Scripture readings. Despite these efforts, skeptics sometimes portray Christians as both unreasonable and unreasoning. As Christians, we sometimes exacerbate the problem when we advocate a definition of "faith" that is removed from evidence altogether. Richard Dawkins once said, "Many of us saw religion as harmless nonsense. Beliefs might lack all supporting evidence but, we thought, if people needed a crutch for consolation, where's the harm? September 11th changed all that."[1]

This view of Christian belief as unreasonable is common among skeptics; unfortunately, it's also common among believers. Critics think Christians accept truth claims without any evidential support, and many Christians embrace the claims of Christianity while unaware of the strong evidence supporting our worldview. Dawkins is correct when he argues against forming beliefs without evidence. People who accept truth claims without any examination of or need for evidence are prone to believing myths and making bad decisions.

Connect the Dots: Consider the evidence from Scripture you've just examined, and take a few moments to reflect on your answers to these questions:

 How can we "examine everything carefully" (1 Thessalonians 5:21 NASB 1995) and "hold on to what is good" (1 Thessalonians 5:21 NIV)?

_____

_____

_____

 Is there something that fully convinced you that Christianity is true?

_____

_____

_____

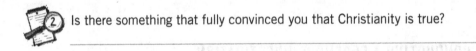 How can we "test the spirits" (1 John 4:1 NIV) to determine whether a spiritual claim is true?

_____

_____

_____

 **MAKING THE CASE**
Diving Deeper into the Evidence

Review the Evidence: This part of the secondary investigation leans heavily on evidence described in the book *Person of Interest*, though you can still consider the material presented here without it. If you have the book, read chapter 1, "The Fuse and the Fallout."

In the video from this week's group investigation, I described the nature of the fuse and the fallout. I talked about the relationship between the *significance* of an event and the *length* of the fuse and the *degree* of the fallout. This is the illustration from the book:

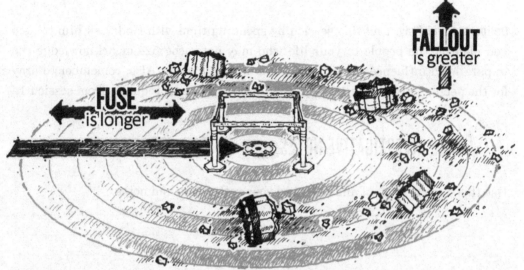

Make an Inference: Given what you remember from the video (or what you read in the book), consider and answer the following questions:

1. What is the relationship between the length of a "fuse" and the degree of "fallout" in any particular event in history?

_____

_____

_____

2. Now consider the appearance of Jesus of Nazareth. What would you expect to find in the fuse and the fallout, given the impact Jesus has had on the lives of so many believers?

_____

_____

_____

"PERSON OF INTEREST"

The term *person of interest* typically refers to someone who has been identified and is involved in a criminal investigation but has not yet been arrested or formally charged with a crime. In criminal terms, it has no legal standing and can refer to either a potential suspect or someone who is cooperating with the investigation and may have helpful information. Steve was our person of interest because he had been suspected of killing Tammy. Jesus became my person of interest because the pastor believed he was something more than a man.

In chapter 1 of *Person of Interest*, I answered this objection: "There is no real evidence for God or Jesus." If someone raised this objection, how would you answer?

_____

_____

_____

_____

Deliberate and Pray: End this session by spending time with God. Ask him to help you identify the people in your life who may not recognize or acknowledge the unparalleled influence Jesus has had on human history. Also, remember to pray for the people in your small group, recalling their prayer requests from session 1.

 ## TAKE INVESTIGATIVE NOTES

Use this page to journal and to record your reflections and notes:

_____

_____

_____

_____

_____

_____

_____

_____

_____

_____

_____

_____

_____

_____

JESUS, THE AVERAGE ANCIENT?

Time brings all things to pass.
—AESCHYLUS

📁 CASE BRIEFING

How often have you heard the expression "timing is everything"? *Opportunity* has been defined as "an appropriate or favorable time or occasion," or "a situation or condition favorable for attainment of a goal."[1] I've investigated homicide cases that went cold years before, only to be reopened decades later. What made the difference? Sometimes a witness decides to come forward. Sometimes the technology has advanced enough to forensically investigate a piece of evidence. As time passes, new opportunities arise, new doors open, and new truths are revealed. *Timing is everything.*

Many years ago, when I was first examining the evidence related to Jesus, my wife, Susie, asked, "So why all the interest in ancient *non*-Christian history?"

"I'm trying to figure out why Jesus appeared *when* he did," I responded.

"I've always wondered about that too," she added. "If Jesus is God, he could've come whenever he wanted, right? Why not come in the time of Moses? Or much later in history, maybe when we had the ability to tell the world about him on the internet?"

"Well, if he's not God, it wouldn't really matter when he arrived." I was a long way from believing in God or considering Christianity as something that mattered. I still saw Jesus as either a work of fiction or a typical ancient sage.

But Susie's questions rang in my ears for several weeks after our conversation, despite my initial response. Was there an aspect of ancient history—a strand of the

"Jesus fuse"—that would identify Jesus as more than an average ancient sage and explain *why* he came when he did?

That's the focus of the next three sessions, beginning with this short examination of the "cultural fuse." Join the rest of your investigative team, and kick off the investigation by briefly engaging one of these questions:

- Why is it hard for most people to be patient for God either to make himself known or to answer prayer?
  —or—
- Why do you think Jesus arrived in history when he did?

 ## OPENING CLUES

Before watching the session 2 video, invite two members of your team to read these verses from the gospel of John:

> On the third day there was a wedding in Cana of Galilee, and the mother of Jesus was there; and both Jesus and His disciples were invited to the wedding. When the wine ran out, the mother of Jesus said to Him, "They have no wine." And Jesus said to her, "What business do you have with Me, woman? My hour has not yet come." His mother said to the servants, "Whatever He tells you, do it." (John 2:1–5)

> After these things Jesus was walking in Galilee, for He was unwilling to walk in Judea because the Jews were seeking to kill Him. Now the feast of the Jews, the Feast of Booths, was near. So His brothers said to Him, "Move on from here and go into Judea, so that Your disciples also may see Your works which You are doing. For no one does anything in secret when he himself is striving to be known publicly. If You are doing these things, show Yourself to the world." For not even His brothers believed in Him. So Jesus said to them, "My time is not yet here, but your time is always ready. The world cannot hate you, but it hates Me because I testify about it, that its deeds are evil. Go up to the feast yourselves; I am not going up to this feast, because My time has not yet fully arrived." Now having said these things to them, He stayed in Galilee. (John 7:1–9)

STATEMENT ANALYSIS

Spend a few minutes reflecting on the verses you just read, then discuss these questions with your group:

> In these verses, Jesus discusses the timing of his public ministry and his eventual path to the cross. Why did Jesus try to control this timing?
>
> What differs between *God's* timing and *our* timing? Why might God pick a specific time in history for Jesus to appear on earth?
>
> How can we discern God's timing in our own lives?

SURVEILLANCE VIDEO

Play the video for session 2. As you watch, use the following section of your investigator's guide to record any thoughts or concepts that stand out to you.

Notes related to Tammy Hayes's no-body homicide case:

_____

_____

_____

_____

_____

Notes related to the history of communication:

_____

_____

_____

_____

_____

_____

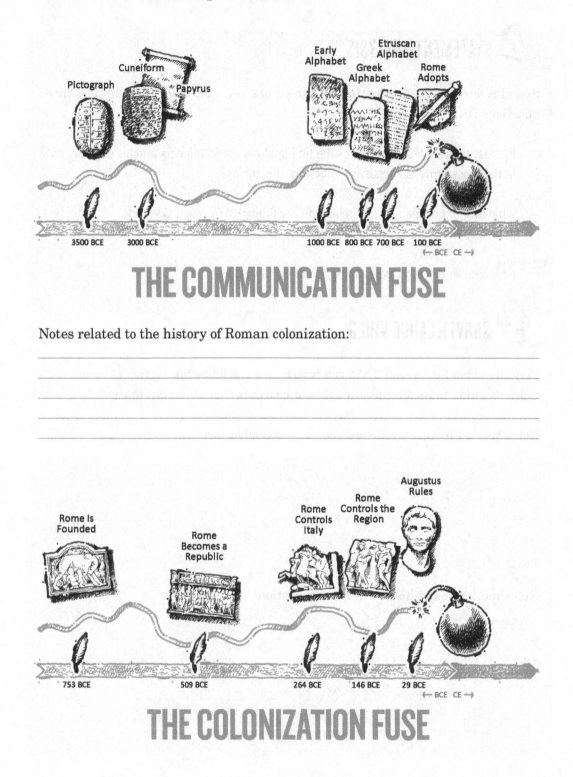

Pictograph

Cuneiform

Papyrus

Early Alphabet

Greek Alphabet

Etruscan Alphabet

Rome Adopts

3500 BCE   3000 BCE   1000 BCE 800 BCE 700 BCE 100 BCE

← BCE   CE →

THE COMMUNICATION FUSE

Notes related to the history of Roman colonization:

_____

_____

_____

_____

_____

Rome Is Founded

Rome Becomes a Republic

Rome Controls Italy

Rome Controls the Region

Augustus Rules

753 BCE   509 BCE   264 BCE   146 BCE   29 BCE

← BCE   CE →

THE COLONIZATION FUSE

Notes related to the history of transportation:

_____

_____

_____

_____

_____

Wheels in Ancient Sumeria — **2-Wheel Carts** — **4-Wheel Wagons** — **Spoke-Wheeled Chariots** — **Royal Road Built by Persians** — **Inferior Greek Road System** — **Romans Build the Appian Way** — **Silk Road Connects to China** — **Romans Build Supporting Roads** — **Romans Build Bridges and Tunnels**

5000 BCE   3000 BCE   2500 BCE   2000 BCE   500 BCE   400 BCE   312 BCE   130 BCE   116 BCE   100 BCE

← BCE   CE →

THE TRANSPORTATION FUSE

Notes related to the history of circulation:

_____

_____

_____

_____

FOLLOW-UP INVESTIGATION

Now that you've watched the video as a group, engage the following questions and discuss what you've just examined with other members of your investigative team:

OBJECTION: WHY DIDN'T JESUS COME LATER IN HISTORY?

If you're active on social media, you probably recognize the crowded, noisy nature of the information age. In addition, technology has advanced to the point that "miraculous" events are easily fabricated in movies and videos. Surveys often find that young people are skeptical and distrusting about many claims made in this environment. Would the message of Jesus be more (or less) likely to resonate in this environment than in the past, when these distractions and innovations were still in the distant future?

Why is the Roman Empire important to the timing of Jesus's arrival? How did the Romans "pave the way" for Jesus and his followers?

_____

_____

_____

_____

_____

 Can God use non-Christians, such as the unbelieving cultures that existed prior to Jesus, to ultimately accomplish his will? If so, how?

_____

_____

_____

_____

Read Acts 14. In this chapter of the book of Acts, Paul and Barnabas are proclaiming Jesus during Paul's first missionary trip. How many cities are described in this short chapter? How did Paul and Barnabas travel from location to location? Describe their efforts and what resulted from their traveling ministry:

_____

_____

_____

_____

_____

Read Acts 24:1–9. Luke records Paul's imprisonment in Caesarea and his trial before Felix the governor. Notice the accusations that are leveled against Paul. They are similar to the allegations made against him elsewhere (see Acts 16:20 and 17:6–7, for example). Given what you now know about the Pax Romana, why would these descriptions of Paul as a "troublemaker" be particularly persuasive to governmental officials?

_____

_____

_____

_____

5 Think about the last time you had a conversation with a young child. What obstacles have you had in trying to explain difficult concepts to someone who can't yet understand some of your vocabulary? How is this similar to the obstacle the ancients had before the development of language and alphabets?

_____

_____

_____

_____

_____

6 **Read 1 Corinthians 16:21; Colossians 4:18; Philemon 19; and 2 Thessalonians 3:17.** Why do you think Paul included these types of statements in many of his letters? **Now read Romans 16:22.** Paul dictated many of his letters to a scribe. Given what you may know about the complexity and depth of Paul's letter to the Romans, why would the development of language and alphabets be important to Paul and his scribes?

_____

_____

_____

_____

7 On Paul's first missionary journey, he used a Roman road (built by Augustus starting in 6 BC) known as the Via Sebaste to travel through Galatia. On his second missionary journey, he used the Via Egnatia to travel from Philippi to Thessalonica. On Paul's journey to Rome, he traveled along the most famous Roman road, the Via Appia. None of these roads would have been available to Paul until the Romans ruled the region. How do you think Jesus's apostles would have communicated the truth about Jesus if an extensive road system weren't in place?

_____

_____

_____

_____

_____

DEBRIEF, DELIBERATE, AND PRAY

Ask God to help you recognize and acknowledge his impact on history and his continuing significance in your own life. Identify the prayer requests of others on your team so you can pray for them this week:

SECONDARY INVESTIGATION

SUMMARIZING THE EVIDENCE

Before you begin this secondary investigation, briefly review your surveillance video notes from session 2. In the space below, write the most significant point(s) you took away from this session.

_____

_____

_____

CONDUCTING A FORENSIC INVESTIGATION
Collecting the Evidence from Scripture

Collect the Evidence: Read Matthew 28:16–20; Mark 16:14–18; Luke 24:44–49; John 20:19–23; and Acts 1:4–8.

Examine the Facts: Many of us feel unprepared (or unqualified) to share Jesus robustly with our friends or family members, even though these passages from Scripture call us, as disciples of Jesus, to make *more* disciples of Jesus. Theologian and Reformation leader Martin Luther once wrote, "If he have faith, the believer cannot be restrained. He betrays himself. He breaks out. He confesses and teaches this gospel to the people at the risk of life itself."[1]

NATURAL AND PROBABLE CONSEQUENCES

According to California Criminal Jury Instructions, a "natural and probable consequence is one that a reasonable person would know is likely to happen if nothing unusual intervenes."[2] In evaluating the cultural fuse leading up to the appearance of Jesus, it is reasonable to ask if Jesus's impact (described in the fallout section) was the inevitable result of the events leading up to his birth or if an unnatural ("unusual") force was involved.

Luther accurately described one of the biggest obstacles to evangelism: *fear*. Many of us are simply afraid to talk about Jesus publicly in a culture that is increasingly skeptical of the Bible. Luther also described the remedy for our fear: *faith*. We sometimes have to "betray" ourselves—step out of our natural inclinations and predispositions—so we can boldly proclaim the gospel.

Connect the Dots: Consider the evidence from Scripture you've just examined, and take a few moments to reflect on your answers to these questions:

 Why do you think the Great Commission of Jesus appears in all four gospels and the book of Acts?

_____

_____

_____

_____

 What are some of the risks people take when declaring the gospel in our culture today?

_____

_____

_____

_____

 Do *you* have fears related to telling others about Jesus? If so, what are they?

_____

_____

_____

_____

 If you have fears about telling others about Jesus, what practical steps can you take to alleviate them and strengthen your resolve to share the truth with others?

_____

_____

_____

_____

MAKING THE CASE
Diving Deeper into the Evidence

Review the Evidence: This part of the secondary investigation leans heavily on the evidence described in the book *Person of Interest*, though you can still consider the material presented here without it. If you have the book, read chapter 2, "Jesus, the Average Ancient?"

Make an Inference: As I described in chapter 2 (and as I described in this week's video session), Roman advancements in road construction and transportation allowed the message of Jesus to advance and spread through the kingdom:

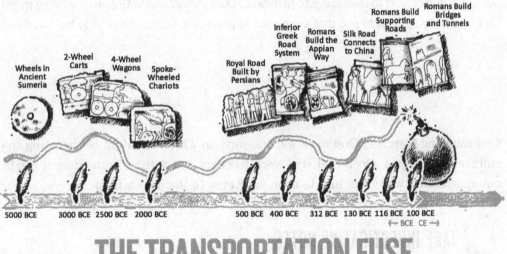

THE TRANSPORTATION FUSE

Connect the Dots: Given what you remember from the video (or what you read in the book), consider and answer the following questions:

1) Can you recall episodes in the book of Acts that describe the important use of roads? Describe as many as you can:

_____

_____

_____

_____

Read Acts 8:26–40. How did God use the road from Jerusalem to Gaza to orchestrate a meeting between Philip and the eunuch? What technological development—aside from the road—was necessary for this encounter to occur? (Refer to the image above or the description of the transportation fuse in chapter 2 of the book):

_____

_____

_____

_____

Read Acts 9:1–9; Acts 22:6–11; and Acts 26:9–20. In the first Bible passage, Luke describes the encounter Saul (the apostle Paul) had with Jesus on the road to Damascus. In the next two passages, Paul also describes his interaction with Jesus. How did God use this road to Damascus to facilitate Paul's conversion to Christianity? Why might God have allowed Saul to use this same road to persecute Christians _prior_ to his salvation?

_____

_____

_____

Deliberate and Pray: Ask God to reveal the ways in which he might be directing the culture around you. Does God still work to shape the future, even when it might not appear that way? Ask him to open your eyes to the possibilities.

TAKE INVESTIGATIVE NOTES

Use this page to journal and to record your reflections and notes:

_____

_____

_____

_____

_____

_____

_____

Session 3

JESUS, THE COPYCAT SAVIOR?

Is man merely a mistake of God's? Or God merely a mistake of man?
—FRIEDRICH NIETZSCHE

CASE BRIEFING

Was there ever a time in your life when you doubted Jesus's existence? Do you know anyone who has questioned the historicity of Jesus?

When I bought and read my first Bible (while I was still a committed atheist), I considered it more akin to mythology than history. As I read the gospel accounts of Jesus, I rejected the supernatural events they alleged as pure fiction. The Gospels appeared to be an ancient work of mythology, and not even *original* mythology at that. The miracle Jesus performed in Cana, for example, was similar to something I read in college—another miracle in which water was turned into wine. That story seemed vaguely familiar, but I remembered a different god performing the miracle: a Greek god known as Dionysus.

According to several ancient myths and sources, Dionysus could create wine from nothing, and water occasionally turned into wine in his presence. The more I thought about it, the more I suspected that Jesus's miracle at Cana had been borrowed from Greek mythology. It wouldn't have been the first time a group had borrowed it; the Romans also adopted the miracles of Dionysus when they renamed him Bacchus and included him in their pantheon of gods.

Why should Jesus matter to me (or to anyone else) if he was nothing more than a "copycat" savior? In this section of our investigation, we'll examine the similarities between Jesus and the mythological deities worshiped in antiquity. Are they similar? And if so, *how* are they alike, and *why* would they share common characteristics?

Before you investigate further, pause for a moment and engage one of these two topics:

- Share one doubt or concern you might have (or might have heard from others) related to the historicity of Jesus or the reliability of the biblical record describing him.

  —or—

- Share what similarities you expect to find between Jesus and the mythological deities of history.

 OPENING CLUES

Before watching this week's surveillance video, invite someone on your team to read aloud the following passage from the Ten Commandments as recorded in the book of Exodus. Listen carefully to the first three directives given by God through Moses:

> God spoke all these words, saying,
>
> "I am the LORD your God, who brought you out of the land of Egypt, out of the house of slavery.
>
> "You shall have no other gods before Me.
>
> "You shall not make for yourself an idol, or any likeness of what is in heaven above or on the earth beneath, or in the water under the earth. You shall not worship them nor serve them; for I, the LORD your God, am a jealous God, inflicting the punishment of the fathers on the children, on the third and the fourth generations of those who hate Me, but showing favor to thousands, to those who love Me and keep My commandments." (Exodus 20:1–6)

Now select someone to read aloud this speech given by Paul in the city of Athens:

> Paul then stood up in the meeting of the Areopagus and said: "People of Athens! I see that in every way you are very religious. For as I walked around and looked carefully at your objects of worship, I even found an altar with this inscription: TO AN UNKNOWN GOD. So you are ignorant of the very thing you worship—and this is what I am going to proclaim to you.

"The God who made the world and everything in it is the Lord of heaven and earth and does not live in temples built by human hands. And he is not served by human hands, as if he needed anything. Rather, he himself gives everyone life and breath and everything else. From one man he made all the nations, that they should inhabit the whole earth; and he marked out their appointed times in history and the boundaries of their lands. God did this so that they would seek him and perhaps reach out for him and find him, though he is not far from any one of us. 'For in him we live and move and have our being.' As some of your own poets have said, 'We are his offspring.'

"Therefore since we are God's offspring, we should not think that the divine being is like gold or silver or stone—an image made by human design and skill. In the past God overlooked such ignorance, but now he commands all people everywhere to repent. For he has set a day when he will judge the world with justice by the man he has appointed. He has given proof of this to everyone by raising him from the dead." (Acts 17:22–31 NIV)

 ## STATEMENT ANALYSIS

Spend a few minutes reflecting on the verses you just read, then discuss these questions with your group:

God clearly knew the Israelites were surrounded by ancient people groups who worshiped deities and myths. Why is God so offended when we worship anything other than him? Why does God describe himself as "jealous"?

The ancient deities and myths were still being worshiped in Paul's day. According to Paul, what are some of the differences between Jesus and the pagan gods being worshiped in Athens? How does Paul demonstrate God's love for the people of Athens?

 ## SURVEILLANCE VIDEO

Play the video for session 3. As you watch, use the following section of your investigator's guide to record any thoughts or concepts that stand out to you.

Notes related to Tammy Hayes's no-body homicide case:

_____

_____

_____

Notes related to the transcendent religious beliefs that humans share (according to recent studies):

_____

_____

_____

Notes related to the fifteen common characteristics of ancient mythologies:

Inevitable:

_____

_____

Imperial:

_____

_____

Inexplicable:

_____

_____

Insulated:

_____

_____

Inveigled:

_____

_____

Identified:

_____

_____

Incredible:

_____

_____

Interactor:

_____

_____

Instructive:

_____

_____

Indemnifier:

_____

_____

Indicted:

_____

_____

Inviter:

_____

_____

Immortal:

_____

_____

Intercessor:

_____

_____

Indicter:

_____

_____

_____

OBJECTION: WHY WOULD GOD REQUIRE A SACRIFICE?

Most ancient religions recognized the imperfect moral nature of humans by requiring a penalty to be paid before believers could appease (or be united with in some way) their god(s). Many of these religions required animal sacrifices to atone for human sin. Christianity did not. Jesus, as God incarnate, paid the price for sin in a way that was different from prior religious systems. Rather than requiring one created being (an animal or human) to die for another, God stepped into history as a human being and paid the price for human sin *on his own*. He replaced the need for repeated sacrifices with a single eternal sacrifice.

Notes related to C. S. Lewis's observation about "true myths":

_____

_____

Notes about Old Testament prophets and leaders who foreshadowed Jesus:

_____

_____

Notes about why Jesus would share some of the characteristics of pagan deities and the characteristics of Old Testament prophets and leaders:

_____

_____

WHY?

FOLLOW-UP INVESTIGATION

Now that you've watched the video as a group, engage the following questions and discuss what you've just learned with the other members of your investigative team:

1. While there are *general* similarities between some ancient myths and Jesus, none are precise matches. Which one of the ancient myth similarities seems most like Jesus? Which common human expectations might account for this similarity?

_____

_____

_____

2) Examine these three attributes of ancient mythologies as a group: inexplicable (the deity entered the world supernaturally), imperial (the deity was part of a royal bloodline), and instructive (the deity eventually teaches human followers). Which common human expectations might account for these similarities?

Inexplicable:

_____

_____

Imperial:

_____

_____

Instructive:

_____

_____

3) **Read Matthew 12:38–41.** Jesus compares himself to Jonah. Work as a team to recall (from the video) the similarities between Jonah and Jesus. What sign does Jesus refer to in this passage? Why would God provide an archetype of Jesus in the person of Jonah? For those who might doubt the story of Jonah and the large fish, why is this statement from Jesus important?

_____

_____

_____

4) **Reread Acts 17:22–28.** Paul quotes two pagan poets in this speech: Cretan philosopher Epimenides ("in him we live and move and have our being") and Cilician Stoic philosopher Aratus ("we are his offspring"). Is Paul's use of ancient *poetry* to point unbelievers to Jesus similar to God's use of ancient *mythology* to point people to Jesus? If so, how?

_____

_____

_____

Read Psalm 96:4–6. The ancient Jews knew they were surrounded by false gods and myths. How is Yahweh different from those gods?

_____

_____

_____

_____

 Think about the ancient non-Jewish deities and Jewish archetypes. Why do you think God eventually entered his creation in a manner that met the expectations and experiences of both groups?

_____

_____

_____

_____

Consider C. S. Lewis's statement about myths:

> Now the story of Christ is simply a *true* myth: a myth working on us in the same way as the others, but with this tremendous difference that it *really happened*: and one must be content to accept it in the same way, remembering that it is *God's* myth where the others are *men's* myths: i.e. the Pagan stories are God expressing Himself through the minds of poets, using such images as He found there, while Christianity is God expressing Himself through what we call "real things."[1] (emphasis mine)

There are two definitions of the word *myth*: (1) "Widely held but false belief(s) or idea(s)," and (2) "a traditional story, especially one concerning the early history of a people or explaining some natural or social phenomenon, and typically involving supernatural beings or events."[2] What does Lewis mean when he describes Jesus as a "true myth"?

_____

_____

_____

_____

_____

 **DEBRIEF, DELIBERATE, AND PRAY**

Ask God to increase your confidence in the truth of the Jesus story, especially when compared with ancient deities. Identify someone in your life who might believe Jesus is a "copycat" savior, and include that person in your prayers, asking God to open an opportunity to share the truth. Identify the prayer requests of others on your team so you can pray for them this week:

Session 3

SECONDARY INVESTIGATION

SUMMARIZING THE EVIDENCE

Before you begin this secondary investigation, briefly review your surveillance video notes from session 3. In the space below, write the most significant point(s) you took away from this session.

_____

_____

_____

CONDUCTING A FORENSIC INVESTIGATION
Collecting the Evidence from Scripture

Collect the Evidence: Read Acts 14:8–18.

Examine the Facts: When we read Bible passages describing the worship of "pagan" gods and deities, it's hard to imagine that we would be similarly tempted to worship "idols," especially in the modern age. But famed nineteenth-century English Baptist preacher Charles Spurgeon once wrote, "Revenge, lust, ambition, pride, and self-will are too often exalted as the gods of man's idolatry; while holiness, peace, contentment, and humility are viewed as unworthy of a serious thought."[1]

Idolatry has been defined as (1) "the worship of a physical object as a god" and (2) "immoderate attachment or devotion to something."[2] The "something" in the second definition doesn't have to be a physical object. As Spurgeon observed, it's possible to be overly attached to our own emotions and desires. In a celebrity-driven culture fueled by social media, it's also possible to worship other humans. How often do we find ourselves adopting an expression or mannerism from a well-known athlete, movie star, or television personality? We emulate and pursue what we worship. Our words, actions, and obsessions reveal our gods.

In this week's session, we read the first three of the Ten Commandments. They described the dangers of idolatry and the jealous nature of God. In this week's secondary investigation Bible reading, Paul and Barnabas attain "celebrity status" and are worshiped as gods. The passage in Acts 14 exposes our human tendency to worship celebrities, even as it reveals God's ability to use our idols to call us to himself.

Connect the Dots: Consider the evidence from Scripture you've just examined, and take a few moments to reflect on your answers to these questions:

 Why did the men of Lystra seek to worship Paul and Barnabas? Why do you think they compared them specifically to Zeus and Hermes? (You may want to do a quick web search for these two gods to get a better sense of their nature and role in the region of present-day Turkey where this took place):

_____

_____

_____

_____

How did Paul and Barnabas compare Zeus and Hermes with the true God of the Bible? What words did they use to describe Zeus and Hermes?

_____

_____

_____

_____

Paul and Barnabas told the crowd, "In past generations He permitted all the nations to go their own ways; yet He did not leave Himself without witness, in that He did good and gave you rains from heaven and fruitful seasons, satisfying your hearts with food and gladness" (Acts 14:16–17). Now that you better understand the common characteristics that ancient deities share, what do you think Paul and Barnabas meant by this statement? How did God leave the pagan nations with a "witness" of his true existence and nature?

_____

_____

_____

_____

MAKING THE CASE
Diving Deeper into the Evidence

Review the Evidence: As in the first two weeks, this part of the secondary investigation leans heavily on evidence described in *Person of Interest*. If you have the book, read chapter 3, "Jesus, the Copycat Savior?"

Make an Inference: In this week's video, I briefly described some of the data that reveal our human inclination to worship a "higher power" of one kind or another. In chapter 3 of the book, I discuss a *New York Times* article by Dr. Preston Greene that describes the work of philosopher Nick Bostrom, who argued that "we might be living in a computer simulation created by a more advanced civilization."[3]

According to Dr. Greene, one way to test the theory is to look for anomalies in the computer simulation. For example, a future scientist might make a mistake in the program that would result in a flaw we might experience today. If this theory is true, a single scientist's error in programing might result in a devastating tornado or in some human misbehavior. Greene warns, however, that we *shouldn't* test the simulation. In fact, he says testing the simulation might anger the future programmers who are watching us: "If our universe has been created by an advanced civilization for research purposes, then it is reasonable to assume that it is crucial to the researchers that we don't find out that we're in a simulation. If we were to prove that we live inside a simulation, this could cause our creators to terminate the simulation—to destroy our world."[4]

Greene has inadvertently revealed yet another example of our innate, human belief in a higher power. Greene imagines a world in which an advanced, creative power (in this case the simulation research team) has the ability to create our world from nothing. He also imagines that human fallenness (in the form of the errant programmer) resulted in the imperfection (the anomalies) we experience in our world. Finally, Greene believes that our creator(s) will ultimately judge us and that we should respect and "fear" them.

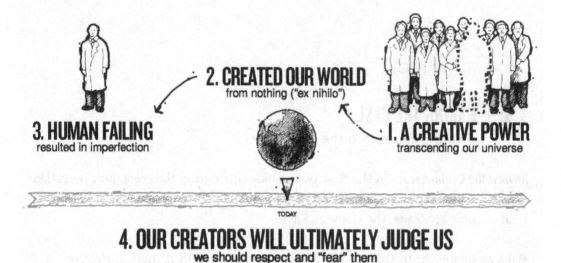

2. CREATED OUR WORLD
from nothing ("ex nihilo")

3. HUMAN FAILING
resulted in imperfection

I. A CREATIVE POWER
transcending our universe

TODAY

4. OUR CREATORS WILL ULTIMATELY JUDGE US
we should respect and "fear" them

Sound familiar? Greene has imagined a new mythology that is obviously similar to many ancient forms of theism. He's simply replaced classic notions of God with updated placeholders. Greene seeks what most humans pursue: an understanding of the Divine.

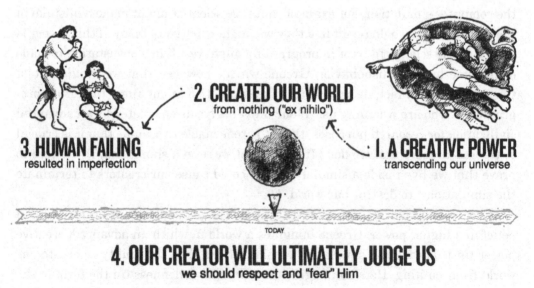

2. CREATED OUR WORLD
from nothing ("ex nihilo")

3. HUMAN FAILING
resulted in imperfection

I. A CREATIVE POWER
transcending our universe

TODAY

4. OUR CREATOR WILL ULTIMATELY JUDGE US
we should respect and "fear" Him

Connect the Dots: Compare the two diagrams above and the similarities between Dr. Greene's assertion and classic Jewish and Christian theism. Given what you remember from the video (or what you read in the book), consider and answer the following questions:

 1 Do you think humans are inclined to think about "higher powers" or spiritual matters? If so, why?

_____

_____

_____

_____

 2 Do you know anyone who claims to be spiritual but not religious? Why does spirituality seem more appealing to some people than specific religious traditions?

_____

_____

_____

_____

OBJECTION: JESUS IS A COPYCAT SAVIOR

Scrutiny of pre-Christian mythologies reveals they are less similar to the story of Jesus Christ than skeptics claim. Cynics typically cherry-pick from the attributes of these myths and exaggerate the alleged similarities to construct a profile vaguely similar to Jesus. It is unreasonable to believe that Christian authors would create a story for Jewish readers by inserting pagan mythological elements into the narrative. More importantly, most alleged similarities are extremely general in nature and would be expected from any group of humans considering the existence of God.

 3 In the book, I claim, "The more the 'expected' meets the expectations of the 'expecter,' the better the response." How could you capitalize on the expectations of others to share the gospel with your friends and family members?

_____

_____

_____

_____

_____

Deliberate and Pray: Ask God to reveal the people in your life who are hesitant to accept the truth about Jesus given his similarities to ancient deities and myths. Ask God for wisdom in reaching these friends, associates, and family members.

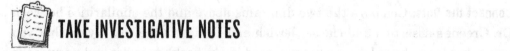

TAKE INVESTIGATIVE NOTES

Use this page to journal and to record your reflections and notes:

Session 4

JESUS, THE MISTAKEN MESSIAH?

Coming events cast their shadows before.
—DORIS LESSING

CASE BRIEFING

It's hard to miss the prophetic references in the four gospel accounts. Mark, Matthew, Luke, and John cited Old Testament prophecies over fifty times when describing Jesus's life, ministry, death, and resurrection. These authors said the Old Testament prophets *predicted* the coming Messiah, and they also claimed Jesus *matched* these predictions.

When I first heard a speaker describe these prophecies, I was . . . underwhelmed.

According to the speaker, over three hundred prophetic predictions clearly identified Jesus as the Jewish Savior. But as I tracked along, many of these prophecies seemed to be less powerful than the speaker claimed.

For example, he claimed, "Isaiah said that the Savior would be beaten on his back, have his beard pulled, and would be spat upon." The speaker cited Isaiah 50:6–7 (ESV):

> I gave my back to those who strike,
>   and my cheeks to those who pull out the beard;
> I hid not my face
>   from disgrace and spitting.
>
> But the Lord GOD helps me;
>   therefore I have not been disgraced;

> therefore I have set my face like a flint,
>
>> and I know that I shall not be put to shame.

As I researched the passage, I found that Jewish believers do not accept it as "messianic," and I could understand why they hesitate to include it. The passage, in a straightforward reading, appears to be a description Isaiah is offering about *himself*, not the future Messiah. Would someone reading this passage *prior* to the arrival of Jesus think Isaiah was referring to the coming Savior? This seems unlikely.

So why do many Christian scholars cite passages such as these, when even Jewish believers don't believe they describe the Messiah? Why did the gospel authors reference similar passages when making their case for Jesus as the Jewish Savior?

Do these Old Testament verses hold any evidential power? Were the ancient Jewish prophets really writing about the Messiah? Was there a prophetic fuse burning toward the explosive appearance of Jesus? That's what we'll investigate in this session.

To jump-start our efforts, gather with your investigative team and briefly engage one of the following:

- If you have one, share which Old Testament prophecy you believe most powerfully demonstrates that Jesus is the Savior.

  —or—

- Share why you think some people are doubtful that the Old Testament prophecies truly point to Jesus.

OPENING CLUES

Before watching the video, select someone to read the following passage from the prophet Isaiah. During the reading, focus on what Isaiah is saying about the nature of prophecy:

> Remember the former things long past,
> For I am God, and there is no other;
> I am God, and there is no one like Me,

Declaring the end from the beginning,
And from ancient times things which have not been done,
Saying, "My plan will be established,
And I will accomplish all My good pleasure."
    (Isaiah 46:9–10, emphasis mine)

Now ask someone to read this verse written by the apostle Peter. In this passage, listen for the role prophecy played at the time this Scripture was written:

As to this salvation, *the prophets who prophesied of the grace that would come* to you made careful searches and inquiries, seeking to know what person or time the Spirit of Christ within them was indicating as He predicted the sufferings of Christ and the glories to follow. (1 Peter 1:10–11, emphasis mine)

STATEMENT ANALYSIS

Spend a few minutes reflecting on the verses you just read, then discuss these questions with your group:

According to Isaiah, the ancient Jews were familiar with God's predictive power. How is that clear from this passage? Why were the ancient Jews interested in a messiah? What kind of savior do you think they expected? How might this expectation have affected their view of Jesus?

According to Peter, why should the Jewish scholars have recognized Jesus as the Messiah? What role did Peter say prophecy should play in identifying the Messiah?

SURVEILLANCE VIDEO

Play the video for session 4. As you watch, use the following section of your investigator's guide to record any thoughts or concepts that stand out to you.

CAN YOU TRUST INFORMANTS?

Investigators must be careful to test their informants. One way to do this is to examine their motives. Jurors are instructed to examine an informant "with caution and close scrutiny."[1] They are told to "consider the extent to which (an informant's statement) may have been influenced by the receipt of, or expectation of, any benefits."[2] What possible motives would ancient Jewish prophets have to lie about the coming Messiah?

Notes related to Tammy Hayes's no-body homicide case:

_____

_____

_____

Notes related to the difference between "clear" and "cloaked" evidence:

_____

_____

_____

Notes related to "reliable" informants:

_____

_____

_____

Notes related to Old Testament prophecies:

_____

_____

_____

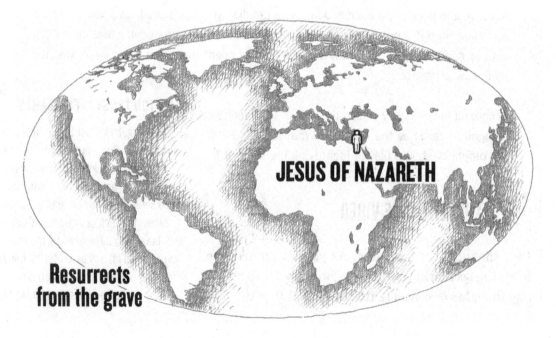

JESUS OF NAZARETH

Resurrects from the grave

Notes related to the uniqueness of Jesus:

_____

_____

_____

 FOLLOW-UP INVESTIGATION

Now that you've finished watching the video, engage the following questions and share your answers with other members of your investigative team:

1 Would the "clear" and "cloaked" distinction help you communicate the value of Old Testament prophecies when communicating the truth about Jesus to others? If so, how?

_____

_____

_____

2 How can the "reliable" informant distinction aid us in isolating the prophecies we use to make the case for Jesus?

_____

_____

_____

3 **Read 2 Peter 1:16–21 and Isaiah 42:1.** Peter begins by recalling his experience at the transfiguration of Jesus, then talks about the nature of prophecy. Isaiah describes a "servant" of God who is being praised in a manner similar to the way Jesus was praised at the transfiguration. What does Peter mean when he wrote that the "prophetic word [was] made more sure" (v. 19)? How did Peter use the words of Isaiah to validate the transfiguration after the fact? Is Peter using the Isaiah passage as clear or cloaked evidence?

_____

_____

_____

4 **Read Acts 1:15–20; Psalm 69:25; and Psalm 109:8.** In the passage from Acts, Peter addresses a group of 120 believers and describes Judas's fate as a fulfillment of Old Testament prophecy as described in these two psalms. Are these two psalms examples of clear or cloaked evidence? Why might these passages from the Psalms be unconvincing to casual readers of the Bible? How might you communicate the nature of clear or cloaked evidence in this situation specifically?

_____

_____

_____

_____

5 **Read Acts 2:14–28.** In this section from his sermon at Pentecost, Peter uses two Old Testament passages, identifying both as prophecy. Which ancient authors does Peter identify as prophets? Are his citations clear or cloaked evidence? Why should this evidence (whether clear or cloaked) have been persuasive to Peter's listeners?

_____

_____

_____

_____

6 Author Peter Stoner (in his book, *Science Speaks*) calculated that the odds of Jesus fulfilling just eight of the Old Testament messianic prophecies was 1 in 100,000,000,000,000,000 (10 to the 17th power).[3] I take a different approach in the video, simply asking how many people would match the rough outline of the Messiah derived from the clear prophecies. Describe the power of either approach.

_____

_____

_____

_____

 Why would God provide predictions about the coming Messiah? _____

_____

_____

_____

DEBRIEF, DELIBERATE, AND PRAY

Ask God to reveal the people in your life who would be most profoundly affected by the Old Testament messianic prophecies. Ask God for wisdom and assistance in remembering the most essential clear prophecies so you can then share them with others. List the people you would like to reach with what you've learned so far. Identify the prayer requests of others on your team so you can pray for them this week:

Session 4

SECONDARY INVESTIGATION

 ## SUMMARIZING THE EVIDENCE

Before you begin this secondary investigation, briefly review your surveillance video notes from session 4. In the following space, write the most significant point(s) you gleaned from this session.

_____

_____

_____

CONDUCTING A FORENSIC INVESTIGATION
Collecting the Evidence from Scripture

Collect the Evidence: Read Deuteronomy 18:17–22; Matthew 7:15–20; 2 Corinthians 11:3–15; and 1 John 4:1–6.

Examine the Facts: History is filled with people who claimed to have the ability to predict the future. Joanna Southcott, for example, was a popular nineteenth-century English "prophetess." In 1813 she predicted she would give birth to the second Messiah but died before this ever happened. Hon-Ming Chen, a twentieth-century Taiwanese religious leader, predicted that God would appear on US television on March 25, 1988, followed by the appearance of devil spirits, flooding, and the mass extinction of all human life. This prophecy also failed to come about. Harold Camping, an American radio broadcaster, predicted the world would end in 1994. When that didn't happen, he predicted a date in 2011.

Southcott, Chen, and Camping could have learned something from the comical proverb, "It is difficult to make predictions, especially about the future."

God provided prophets who predicted the coming of the Jewish Messiah with clear and cloaked evidence. God also knew there would be many *false* prophets. That's why the biblical authors repeatedly warned us about false teachers and God provided us with a way to test those who claim to be prophets.

Connect the Dots: Reflect on the evidence from Scripture you've just examined, and take a few moments to consider your answers to these questions:

  How does Moses say we can identify a true prophet (in Deuteronomy 18:17–22)?

_____

_____

_____

How does Jesus say we can identify false teachers (in Matthew 7:15–20)?

_____

_____

_____

How do Paul and John describe false teachers (in 2 Corinthians 11:3–15 and 1 John 4:1–6)? Whom do Paul and John associate with false prophets, and why do they make this association?

_____

_____

_____

MAKING THE CASE
Diving Deeper into the Evidence

Review the Evidence: This part of the secondary investigation leans heavily on evidence described in *Person of Interest*. If you have the book, read chapter 4, "Jesus, the Mistaken Messiah?"

Make an Inference: I referenced Daniel's prediction (recorded in Daniel 9) that provides us with a time frame in which the Jewish person of interest would appear in history. This time frame has clear beginning and ending points: "So you are to know and understand that from the issuing of a decree to restore and rebuild Jerusalem, until Messiah the Prince, there will be seven weeks and sixty-two weeks; it will be built again, with streets and moat, even in times of distress. Then after the sixty-two weeks, the Messiah will be cut off and have nothing, and the people of the prince who is to come will destroy the city and the sanctuary" (Daniel 9:25–26).

In 586 BCE Daniel predicted a future decree to rebuild Jerusalem. According to the Old Testament, the decree to restore and rebuild Jerusalem was issued "in the month Nisan, in the twentieth year of King Artaxerxes" (Nehemiah 2:1), which is March 5, 444 BCE, according to our Julian calendar. Daniel also prophesied that "the people of the prince who is to come will destroy the city and the sanctuary" (Daniel 9:26). This did ultimately occur when the temple was destroyed in 70 CE.

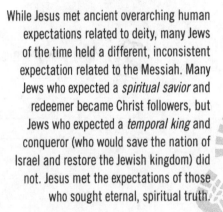

OBJECTION: WHY DIDN'T FIRST-CENTURY JEWS RECOGNIZE JESUS AS THE MESSIAH?

While Jesus met ancient overarching human expectations related to deity, many Jews of the time held a different, inconsistent expectation related to the Messiah. Many Jews who expected a *spiritual savior* and redeemer became Christ followers, but Jews who expected a *temporal king* and conqueror (who would save the nation of Israel and restore the Jewish kingdom) did not. Jesus met the expectations of those who sought eternal, spiritual truth.

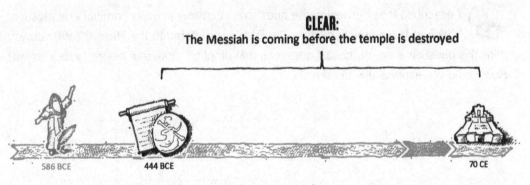

CLEAR:
The Messiah is coming before the temple is destroyed

586 BCE　　444 BCE　　70 CE

A Messiah is coming to make atonement 173,880 days AFTER a decree is issued to rebuild Jerusalem. He will then be "cut off" and "have nothing" sometime BEFORE Jerusalem and the temple are destroyed.

Connect the Dots: Given what you remember from the video (or what you read in the book), consider and answer the following questions:

1 Is Daniel a reliable informant? Which historical events—aside from the appearance of the Messiah—did Daniel accurately predict? How could you share these facts with others?

_____

_____

_____

_____

_____

 2 Write how you might express what Daniel predicted about the coming of Jesus:

_____

_____

_____

_____

_____

3 I described the six investigative questions I consider in every criminal investigation. Which of these questions does Daniel answer related to the Messiah? Why do you think this question is one of the last questions that prophets answered before Jesus's arrival? How would you express this to others?

_____

_____

_____

_____

_____

Deliberate and Pray: Ask God to continue to strengthen your confidence in Jesus as our Savior. Ask him to motivate you to reach those in your world who would benefit from what you've learned, and ask God to specifically identify people by name.

TAKE INVESTIGATIVE NOTES

Use this page to journal and to record your reflections and notes:

Session 5

IN THE FULLNESS OF TIME

It is the mark of a good action that it appears inevitable in retrospect.
—ROBERT LOUIS STEVENSON

📁 CASE BRIEFING

I still remember buying our first new car. The circumstances in our lives aligned perfectly to make the purchase both possible and necessary. I had recently completed my university education and landed a stable job. I had also just received a pay increase. The added income provided an opportunity that was previously unavailable to us.

We also faced a deadline of sorts. We had a second baby on the way, and we were quickly outgrowing the small car I used to commute to school.

We were prepared to buy a used minivan when a new car dealership opened and ran a promotional deal on an entry-level SUV. The timing couldn't have been better. We acted quickly within this narrow range of opportunity (before the sale expired) to purchase our first new car.

In this session, you'll learn that these limited windows of opportunity have a *name*, at least in my criminal investigations. I call them "red zones." A red zone is a period of time when the opportunity to commit a crime presents itself. Every red zone is unique to the killer and his or her situation. A red zone lies at the end of the fuse that burns toward the explosive commission of each crime, and it usually helps identify the killer and explain their motives.

This week your investigative team will examine two red zones: one for the Tammy Hayes case and another for the explosive inauguration of the Common Era. You may be surprised to discover what these red zones reveal. There's a reason why our calendar has been divided into BCE (BC) and CE (AD), and this reason is obvious from the red zones that resulted from the spiritual, cultural, and prophetic fuses we've already examined.

Before you go any further as a group, take a minute to briefly engage one of the following:

- Share one example in your own life when a narrow window of opportunity presented itself.
    —or—
- Share why you think some people prefer the dating system using BCE and CE terminology instead of BC and AD.

OPENING CLUES

Before watching the video, select one member of your team to read aloud the following verse from King Solomon. Note what he said about God's work:

> He has made everything appropriate in its time. He has also set eternity in their heart, without the possibility that mankind will find out the work which God has done from the beginning even to the end. (Ecclesiastes 3:11)

Now select another member to read aloud what Jesus said to his disciples. Note what he said about God's timing:

> When they had come together, they began asking Him, saying, "Lord, is it at this time that You are restoring the kingdom to Israel?" But He said to them, "It is not for you to know periods of time or appointed times which the Father has set by His own authority; but you will receive power when the Holy Spirit has come upon you; and you shall be My witnesses both in Jerusalem and in all Judea, and Samaria, and as far as the remotest part of the earth." (Acts 1:6–8)

STATEMENT ANALYSIS

Spend a few minutes reviewing the verses you just read, then discuss these questions as a group:

What did Solomon mean when he wrote that God "set eternity" in our hearts? Why would God keep his plan hidden so that humankind couldn't "find out the work which God has done"? How might this second part of the verse explain why the spiritual, cultural, and prophetic fuses weren't more obvious to the ancients?

Jesus said it was not for us to know the periods of time or appointed times set by the Father. Why would God want it this way? Why are humans so interested in determining God's timing, *despite* these admonitions?

SURVEILLANCE VIDEO

Play the video for session 5. As you watch, use the following section of your investigator's guide to record any thoughts or concepts that stand out to you.

Notes related to Tammy Hayes's red zone:

_____

_____

_____

_____

_____

the RED zone

The crime (if it occurs in our city) would happen here

January 2000

Auto shop opens

April 2000

Steve and Tammy move to our city

Notes related to the ancient spiritual red zone:

_____

_____

_____

_____

_____

_____

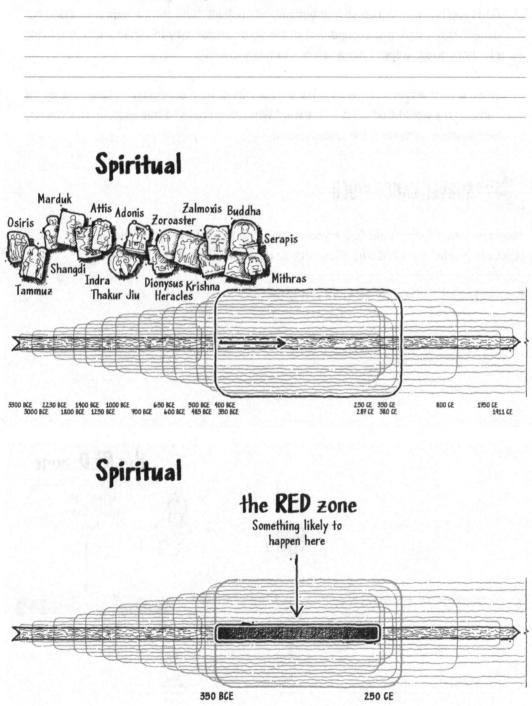

Notes related to the ancient cultural red zone:

_____

_____

_____

_____

_____

_____

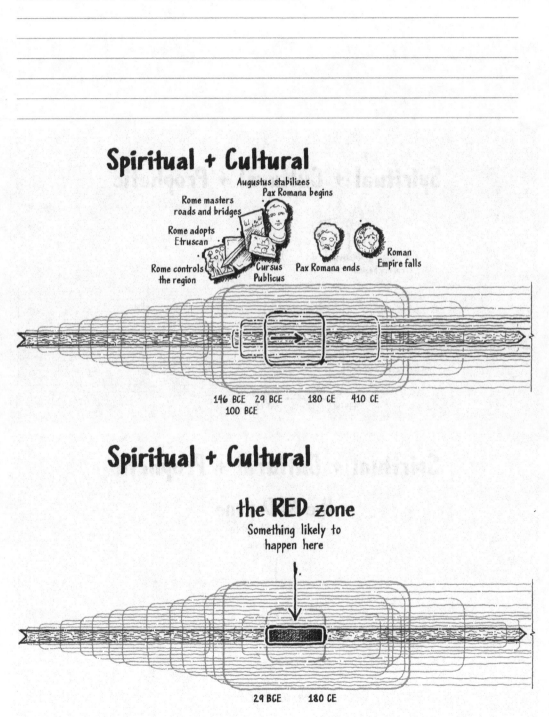

Spiritual + Cultural

Rome masters
roads and bridges

Augustus stabilizes
Pax Romana begins

Rome adopts
Etruscan

Rome controls
the region

Cursus
Publicus

Pax Romana ends

Roman
Empire falls

146 BCE   29 BCE   180 CE   410 CE
100 BCE

Spiritual + Cultural

the RED zone
Something likely to
happen here

29 BCE   180 CE

Notes related to the ancient prophetic red zone:

_____
_____
_____
_____
_____
_____

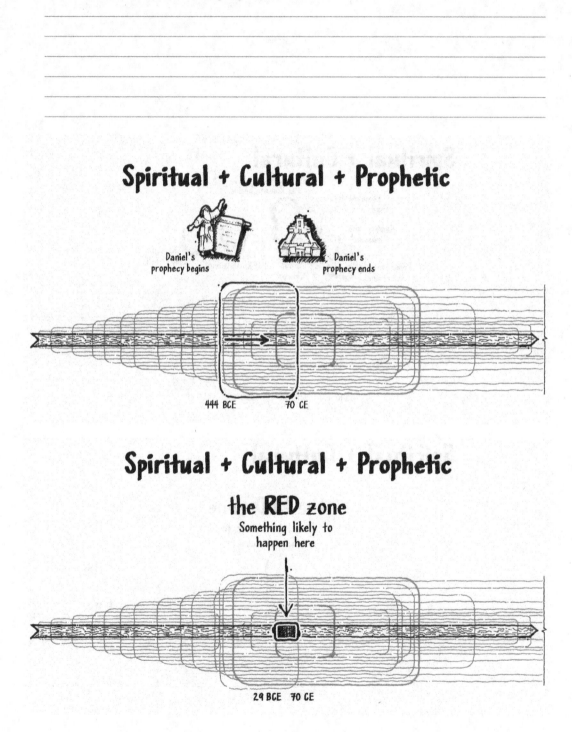

Spiritual + Cultural + Prophetic

Daniel's prophecy begins

Daniel's prophecy ends

444 BCE   70 CE

Spiritual + Cultural + Prophetic

the RED zone

Something likely to happen here

29 BCE   70 CE

Notes related to the explanation of the red zone:

_____

_____

_____

_____

 ## FOLLOW-UP INVESTIGATION

Now that you've watched the video as a group, engage the following questions and discuss what you've just examined with other members of your investigative team:

(1) Why is God's timing better than ours?

_____

_____

_____

(2) Do you think God uses regular people, nations, and human authorities to eventually accomplish his will? If so, how?

_____

_____

_____

_____

 (3) **Read Galatians 4:4–5.** Given what you've just learned about the historic red zone, what do you think Paul meant by the "fullness of time"? What factors made the red zone the perfect time for Jesus's arrival?

_____

_____

_____

_____

Read 1 Timothy 6:11–16. Paul is writing to Timothy to encourage him to avoid the temptations of money and worldly possessions. What does Paul say about the timing of Jesus's return? What can we infer about the *first* appearance of Jesus from this description of God's involvement in Jesus's *second* appearance?

_____

_____

_____

_____

_____

 Read Habakkuk 2:1–3. In this passage, God tells the prophet Habakkuk to write down his vision on tablets. What does God mean when he says, "The vision awaits its appointed time" (ESV)?

_____

_____

_____

_____

_____

 The God of the Bible is described as all-powerful, all-loving, and all-knowing. If this is true, why is waiting on his timing in our lives often so hard?

_____

_____

_____

_____

_____

_____

What specific aspects of our present culture do you think God is using to prepare the future coming of Jesus?

_____

_____

_____

_____

_____

 ## DEBRIEF, DELIBERATE, AND PRAY

Pray as a team before you close your time together. Ask God to help you submit your plans to his plan. Ask him to give you the patience and wisdom to trust his timing rather than yours. Jot down the areas of your life where you need to be more patient. Identify the prayer requests of others on your team so you can pray for them this week:

Session 5

SECONDARY INVESTIGATION

 ## SUMMARIZING THE EVIDENCE

Before you begin this secondary investigation, briefly review your surveillance video notes from session 5. Use this space to write the most significant point(s) you want to remember from this session.

_____

_____

_____

CONDUCTING A FORENSIC INVESTIGATION
Collecting the Evidence from Scripture

Collect the Evidence: Read Romans 5:1–6; 2 Peter 3:8–9; and Lamentations 3:25–26.

Examine the Facts: Most of us know someone who has yet to accept the salvation Jesus offers. Have you been praying for someone and wondering why God hasn't yet acted to bring this person to faith in Christ? God's timing in salvation is often hard to comprehend on this side of eternity. It's difficult to understand why our unsaved friends and family members won't accept Jesus as Lord. George Whitefield, an Anglican evangelist (and one of the founders of Methodism), once preached, "Now let me address all of you, high and low, rich and poor, one with another, to accept of mercy and grace while it is offered to you; 'now is the accepted time, now is the day of salvation'; and will you not accept it, now it is offered unto you?"[1]

Why do some of us understand that "*now* is the accepted time, *now* is the day of salvation" (emphasis mine)? Why do some people reject the gospel, while others respond in a timely manner?

Connect the Dots: Consider the evidence from Scripture you've just examined, and take a few moments to reflect on your answers to these questions:

 ① In Romans 5:1–6, Paul describes how Jesus died for the ungodly. Why do you think Paul wrote that Jesus died "at the *right* time" (my emphasis)?

_____

_____

_____

② In 2 Peter 3:8–9, Peter describes the difference between the way we experience time and the way God experiences it. Does this help explain why God might delay the salvation of those we love? If so, how?

_____

_____

_____

③ In Lamentations 3:25–26, Jeremiah describes those who wait patiently for God's timing. Why is it good to wait "silently for the salvation of the LORD," even if it involves the salvation of those we have been praying for?

_____

_____

_____

MAKING THE CASE
Diving Deeper into the Evidence

Review the Evidence: As before, this part of the secondary investigation leans heavily on evidence described in *Person of Interest*. If you have the book, read chapter 5, "In the Fullness of Time."

Make an Inference: The three-stranded fuse that burned toward the Common Era seemed to make Jesus's arrival inevitable. He met our human expectations, matched the Jewish predictions, and arrived at precisely the right time in the history of the Roman Empire to be shared with the entire known world.

Person of Interest?
BCE   CE

Jesus arrived in God's timing. Author Gail Godwin once wrote, "Some things arrive on their own mysterious hour, on their own terms and not yours, to be seized or relinquished forever."[2]

Connect the Dots: Think back to what you remember from the video (or what you read in the book) to answer the following questions:

 1) What, in your mind, is the most interesting or powerful aspect of the "red zone" created by the spiritual, cultural, and prophetic fuses?

_____

_____

_____

2) Write down how you would summarize and share with someone the evidence for the red zone and why it points to Jesus:

_____

_____

_____

 3) What would you say to someone who claims Jesus appears in this red zone only coincidentally?

_____

_____

_____

Deliberate and Pray: Ask God to continue to reveal people with whom you can share the truth about Jesus and the salvation he offers. Ask him for patience as you wait on his timing. Ask him to strengthen your character so you can model Jesus to your friends and family as you wait.

TAKE INVESTIGATIVE NOTES

Use this page to journal and to record your reflections and notes:

Session 6

JESUS, THE UNFOUNDED FICTION?

Books are the carriers of civilization. Without books,
history is silent, literature dumb, science crippled,
thought and speculation at a standstill. Without books,
the development of civilization would have been impossible.
—BARBARA TUCHMAN

 **CASE BRIEFING**

At the time of his death, Elvis Presley had more No. 1 albums than any other male recording artist in history. Even today, Elvis remains the second "Richest Dead Celebrity" (with over one billion albums sold, earning $39 million in 2019 alone). In the four decades after his passing, hundreds of books were written about Elvis's extravagant career and tragic death.

Authors seeking to retell the story of Elvis typically fall into one of three groups:

1. Presleys (family members and close friends) who liked Elvis
2. Non-Presleys (strangers) who liked Elvis
3. Non-Presleys (strangers) who disliked Elvis

The truthfulness of these Elvis books is closely tied to which of the three groups the author belongs. Some authors favored Elvis; some did not. Some were close to Elvis; some were not. Some were accurate; some were not. You might wonder how someone could write something *untrue* about Elvis and get away with it, but remember, Elvis died in 1977, long before the internet turned the world into an accessible, global community. Unless you happened to live in Elvis's hometown

(Memphis, Tennessee), you were probably unlikely to bump into true eyewitnesses who could verify the claims of an author. In addition, some of these Elvis books were written long after living witnesses could fact-check them. As a result, truth and legend emerged, the latter more likely from the pen of someone with a bias as distance and time increased.

Even though a wild variety of fables and tales were written about Elvis, they were crafted upon common features of the *true* Elvis story. Every "tall-tale" *distortion* of Elvis borrows from the truth of the *real* Elvis, an Elvis who really existed, even though late, embellished accounts may exaggerate or misstate the truth. When someone has the kind of cultural impact Elvis had, we should expect there to be significant fallout, including literature written by people who would distort the truth and even co-opt his story for their own advantage.

Something similar happened to Jesus, thousands of years before Elvis ever recorded "Heartbreak Hotel."

In this session, your investigative team will explore the incredible impact Jesus had on literature as you begin to examine the fallout of the Common Era. Kick off this investigation by briefly engaging one of the following topics:

- Share your interests in literature with the group, describing your preferences for fiction or nonfiction.

  —or—

- Share the latest book you've read about Jesus and the impact it had on you.

OPENING CLUES

Before watching the next surveillance video, pick someone to read these verses from John's gospel:

Many other signs Jesus also performed in the presence of the disciples, which are not written in this book; but these have been written so that you may believe that Jesus is the Christ, the Son of God; and that by believing you may have life in His name. (John 20:30–31)

Now read this additional passage, focusing on what John said about the futility of trying to capture in writing everything Jesus did:

This is the disciple who is testifying about these things and wrote these things, and we know that his testimony is true.

But there are also many other things which Jesus did, which, if they were written in detail, I expect that even the world itself would not contain the books that would be written. (John 21:24–25)

STATEMENT ANALYSIS

Spend a few minutes reflecting on the verses as a team, then discuss these questions with your group:

The disciples (John included) clearly left much of what Jesus did *undocumented*. Why did they pick some episodes for inclusion and leave others out? Why do many still consider the Gospels a reliable record of Jesus's life and ministry if it doesn't include every detail?

The disciples realized the impossibility of trying to capture every piece of evidence related to Jesus. Why might modern authors find it even *more* difficult to capture every inference and theological truth about Jesus? Why do books about Jesus continue to be written?

SURVEILLANCE VIDEO

Play the video for session 6. As you watch, use this portion of your investigator's guide to record any thoughts or concepts that stand out to you.

Notes related to Tammy Hayes's no-body homicide case:

_____

_____

_____

Notes related to the writings of Christians who liked Jesus:

_____

_____

_____

Notes related to the writings of non-Christians who liked Jesus:

_____
_____
_____
_____
_____
_____

Notes related to the writings of non-Christians who disliked Jesus:

_____
_____
_____
_____
_____
_____

Notes related to books and screenplays written about Jesus:

_____
_____
_____
_____
_____
_____

Notes related to "Christ figures" in literature:

_____

_____

_____

_____

FOLLOW-UP INVESTIGATION

Now that you've watched the video as a group, engage the following questions and discuss what you've just examined with other members of your investigative team:

1 Why is it important to demonstrate that Jesus's life can be robustly reconstructed from the writings of Christians who liked Jesus, non-Christians who liked Jesus, and non-Christians who disliked Jesus?

_____

_____

_____

_____

OBJECTION: THERE ISN'T ENOUGH ANCIENT, NON-CHRISTIAN INFORMATION ABOUT JESUS

If you include the noncanonical texts, there are nearly twice as many non-Christian voices as Christian voices in the period preceding the Edict of Milan. In addition, the ancient sources we have for the life and ministry of Jesus are more reliable (and were written much earlier) than the sources we have for the life of Tiberius Caesar, the emperor of Rome who ruled during the latter part of Jesus's lifetime. Some of these sources (like Tacitus), report on both men. If we have enough information to have knowledge about Tiberius Caesar, then we have enough information to have knowledge about Jesus.

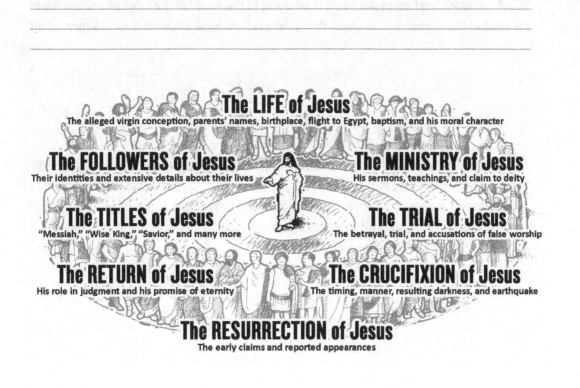

The LIFE of Jesus
The alleged virgin conception, parents' names, birthplace, flight to Egypt, baptism, and his moral character

The FOLLOWERS of Jesus
Their identities and extensive details about their lives

The MINISTRY of Jesus
His sermons, teachings, and claim to deity

The TITLES of Jesus
"Messiah," "Wise King," "Savior," and many more

The TRIAL of Jesus
The betrayal, trial, and accusations of false worship

The RETURN of Jesus
His role in judgment and his promise of eternity

The CRUCIFIXION of Jesus
The timing, manner, resulting darkness, and earthquake

The RESURRECTION of Jesus
The early claims and reported appearances

Why is the reconstruction of Jesus's life from non-Christians who disliked Jesus particularly important?

_____

_____

_____

_____

 Read Acts 17:10–12. Luke is describing the people of Berea and the way they examined the claims related to Jesus. Does God place value in the practice of reading and studying? Why might God continue to bless human efforts to write about Jesus?

_____

_____

_____

_____

Read Ecclesiastes 12:9–13. King Solomon writes, "the writing of many books is endless, and excessive study is wearying to the body" (v. 12). Does Solomon reject the value of literature in this passage? Why or why not? In verse 13, what does Solomon value?

_____

_____

_____

_____

Read 1 Timothy 4:12–14. In this passage, Paul provides direction for young Timothy and admonishes him to continue "public reading" (v. 13). What kind of literature do you think Paul wanted Timothy to read publicly? Why might this sort of activity allay concerns about Timothy's youthfulness? How might the continued reading of books about Jesus contribute to *our* wisdom and maturity?

_____

_____

_____

_____

Why has Jesus been the topic of so many screenplays? Why is the Jesus story so enduring?

_____

_____

_____

_____

Why do many authors craft their protagonists to resemble Jesus? How might non-Christians explain this phenomenon?

_____

_____

_____

_____

🙏 DEBRIEF, DELIBERATE, AND PRAY

Pray as a team before you close your time together. Ask God to open your eyes to the classic literature describing Jesus (or the worldview he inaugurated). Ask God to guide you to wise choices as you continue to read about Jesus of Nazareth and to build your confidence in the truth of Christianity. Identify the prayer requests of others on your team so you can pray for them this week:

_____

_____

_____

_____

_____

_____

_____

_____

_____

Session 6

SECONDARY INVESTIGATION

SUMMARIZING THE EVIDENCE

Before you begin this secondary investigation, briefly review your surveillance video notes from session 6. In the space below, write the most significant takeaway(s).

_____

_____

_____

CONDUCTING A FORENSIC INVESTIGATION
Collecting the Evidence from Scripture

Collect the Evidence: Read 1 Timothy 5:17–18; Luke 10:7; 1 Corinthians 11:23–25; and Luke 22:19–20.

Examine the Facts: When I was an atheist, I believed that the Gospels were penned in the second century (at the earliest) and were written too late to be true eyewitness accounts. I rejected the idea that Jesus followers first wrote about Jesus within the lifetime of the eyewitnesses. I resonated with people like Géza Vermes, the skeptical scholar and historian who once wrote, "The so-called Gospel of John is something special and reflects . . . the highly evolved theology of a Christian writer who lived three generations after Jesus."[1]

OBJECTION: YOU CAN'T TRUST OLD MEMORIES

Jurors can evaluate witnesses to determine how well they "remember and describe what happened."[2] But how can a witness be trusted when their testimony occurs *many years* after an event took place? Remember that not all events leave the same impression on witnesses. Some events (such as Spencer's phone call to Tammy's husband) are more memorable than others. Jurors are told to consider the importance of a memory when evaluating the witness. In a similar way, the gospel accounts, even though they were written about Jesus many years after the fact, recall events that were highly unusual and memorable.

75

But as I later discovered, the followers of Jesus began writing about him within the very first generation of eyewitnesses. The verses you just read demonstrate this truth.

Connect the Dots: Consider the biblical evidence you've just examined, and take a few moments to reflect on your answers to these questions:

 1. In the passage from 1 Timothy (written around 63–65 CE), Paul is aware of Luke's gospel and wrote as though it was common knowledge. Paul quotes two passages as "Scripture" here—one in the Old Testament and one in the New. "You shall not muzzle the ox while it is threshing" refers to Deuteronomy 25:4, and "The laborer is worthy of his wages" refers to Luke 10:7. What does Paul's reference to Luke's gospel tell us about how early it was written?

_____

_____

_____

_____

2. In the passage from 1 Corinthians, penned between 53–57 CE (even earlier than 1 Timothy), Paul once again references Luke's gospel, citing Luke 22:19–20. Luke's gospel is the only text where Jesus says that the disciples are to eat the bread and drink the wine "in remembrance of me." What does Paul's inclusion of this verse tell us about the date of Luke's gospel? How early do you think people started writing about Jesus?

_____

_____

_____

_____

3. Why do many skeptics argue for the late dating of the Gospels when there is evidence they were written early?

_____

_____

_____

_____

_____

MAKING THE CASE
Diving Deeper into the Evidence

Review the Evidence: This part of the secondary investigation leans heavily on evidence described in *Person of Interest*. If you have the book, read chapter 6, "Jesus, the Unfounded Fiction?"

Make an Inference: Perhaps the most surprising literary genre that Jesus affected in the Common Era fallout has been in the category of screenplays. As visual technology progressed, this new category of literature emerged. From the very invention of the "moving picture," Jesus became the focus of writers who were inspired by his impact on culture.

Some of the earliest attempts to create motion pictures featured the life of Jesus. In 1897, for example, Albert Kirchner filmed *La Passion du Christ*, while Mark Klaw and Abraham Erlanger created *The Horitz Passion Play*. These primitive films started an explosion of cinematic activity depicting Jesus's life:

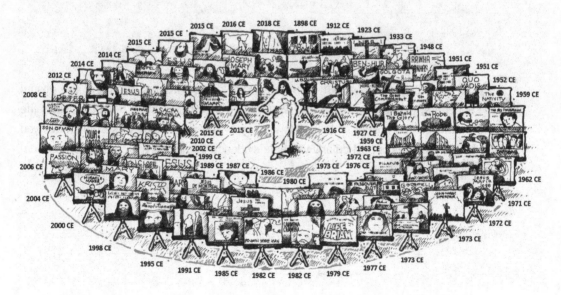

No other religious figure has inspired as many screenplays as Jesus of Nazareth, and this doesn't even include any of the movies that reflect a Christian worldview but don't specifically reenact Jesus's life, ministry, death, and resurrection. Hundreds more have been written describing the lives and experiences of his followers.

Connect the Dots: Given what you viewed in this week's surveillance video (or what you read in the book), consider and answer the following questions:

 (1) Which movies about Jesus have you seen? Which was your favorite, and why? Whom might you invite to watch one of these movies?

_____

_____

_____

_____

(2) Movies about Jesus have been produced in a variety of countries, including Bulgaria, Canada, England, France, Germany, India, Iran, Italy, Jordan, Lebanon, Mexico, Israel, the Philippines, Portugal, South Africa, Spain, and the United States. Why is Jesus such a global phenomenon?

_____

_____

_____

_____

(3) Some of the movies about Jesus are word-for-word reenactments of the gospel accounts, including *The Jesus Film* (created in 1979), which depicts Jesus's life based primarily on the gospel of Luke. How many of these verse-by-verse films have you seen? Why are these films particularly valuable evidence in making the case for Jesus from the Common Era fallout?

_____

_____

_____

_____

Deliberate and Pray: Ask God to identify someone in your life who could benefit from what you've just learned, and ask him to give you the wisdom and words to communicate the truth to that person. Ask for opportunities to share a gospel movie with someone who hasn't yet seen one.

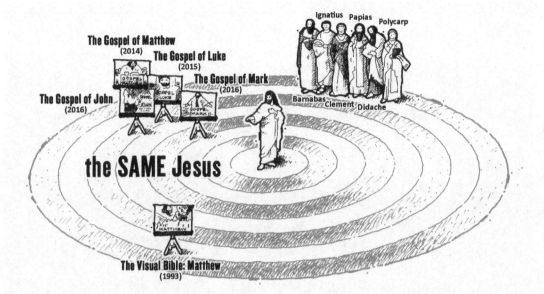

TAKE INVESTIGATIVE NOTES

Use this page to journal and to record your reflections and notes:

_____

_____

_____

_____

_____

_____

_____

_____

_____

_____

_____

_____

_____

_____

_____

_____

_____

_____

_____

_____

Session 7

JESUS, THE DREARY DEITY?

Today, from countless paintings, statues, and buildings,
from literature and history, from personality and institution,
from profanity, popular song, and entertainment media, from confession
and controversy, from legend and ritual—Jesus stands quietly at
the center of the contemporary world, as he himself predicted.
—DALLAS WILLARD

 CASE BRIEFING

Before becoming a detective, I earned two degrees in the arts (in design and architecture). As a young man, I was obsessed with the visual arts and with the history of architecture.

The year I graduated with my design degree, I traveled to Europe and visited some of the best examples of artistry the world has ever seen. This trip included a visit to Ottobeuren Abbey, a Benedictine monastery in Southern Germany. It was founded in 764 CE and includes a magnificent basilica that has been described as the "pinnacle of Bavarian Baroque architecture."[1] The interior is nothing short of breathtaking, covered in paintings and housing a magnificent pipe organ above the narthex. Jesus followers have been meeting in this space for centuries, admiring the art and singing to the accompaniment of organ music.

Their experience hasn't been unusual. Christians have been meeting in this way for two thousand years, although they haven't always enjoyed this kind of artistic grandeur. Instead, the early Christians met in simple homes.

The evolution of Christian church architecture—and the art that ordained the walls of cathedrals and basilicas across the globe—served as a catalyst for the

81

visual arts and music. This robust contribution is yet another part of the Common Era fallout caused by Jesus of Nazareth and his followers.

In this session, we'll investigate the impact Jesus had on the arts and demonstrate yet another way in which the story of Jesus can be reconstructed, even if every page of Christian Scripture were destroyed.

But before your group begins, share some information with each other from one of these two suggestions:

- Share your favorite form of visual art (for example, painting, sketching, sculpture, and so on) and any experience you might have participating in this art form.
    —or—
- Share about one of your favorite Christian singers, bands, or worship leaders. What makes their contribution to the arts so powerful?

OPENING CLUES

Before watching the video this week, invite someone to read aloud the following Old Testament passage describing the way God instructed Moses to adorn the tent of meeting:

The LORD spoke to Moses, saying, "See, I have called by name Bezalel, the son of Uri, the son of Hur, of the tribe of Judah. And I have filled him with the Spirit of God in wisdom, in understanding, in knowledge, and in all kinds of craftsmanship, to create artistic designs for work in gold, in silver, and in bronze, and in the cutting of stones for settings, and in the carving of wood, so that he may work in all kinds of craftsmanship. And behold, I Myself have appointed with him Oholiab, the son of Ahisamach, of the tribe of Dan; and in the hearts of all who are skillful I have put skill, so that they may make everything that I have commanded you: the tent of meeting, the ark of testimony, the atoning cover that is on it, and all the furniture of the tent, the table and its utensils, the pure gold lampstand with all its utensils, and the altar of incense, the altar of burnt offering with all its utensils, and the basin and its stand, the woven garments as well: the holy garments for Aaron the priest and the garments of his sons, with which to carry out their priesthood; the anointing oil also, and the fragrant incense for the Holy Place, they are to make them according to everything that I have commanded you." (Exodus 31:1–11)

Now ask another volunteer to read this passage:

> The sons of the Levites carried the ark of God on their shoulders with the poles on them, just as Moses had commanded in accordance with the word of the LORD.
>
> Then David spoke to the chiefs of the Levites to appoint their relatives as the singers, with musical instruments, harps, lyres, and cymbals, playing to raise sounds of joy. (1 Chronicles 15:15–16)

STATEMENT ANALYSIS

Spend a few minutes reflecting on the verses you just read, then discuss these questions with your group:

From the first passage, what kinds of artistic elements did God require for the tabernacle and the Tent of Meeting? What is special about Oholiab? How are artists especially gifted by God?

From the second passage, why do you think music is important to God? Why would he appoint members of the Levites (typically reserved for service to God in the tabernacle or the temple) to perform musically?

SURVEILLANCE VIDEO

Play the video for session 7. As you watch, use the following section of your investigator's guide to record any thoughts or concepts that stand out to you.

Notes related to Tammy Hayes's no-body homicide case:

_____

_____

_____

_____

_____

OBJECTION: CHRISTIAN ART IS INFERIOR TO SECULAR ART

Perhaps you've heard people complain that Christian art, music, or movies are somehow inferior when compared with contemporary secular movies and artists. Without examining specific examples, one thing is certain: some of the greatest art and music in history has been inspired by Jesus and created by Jesus followers. Jesus is not an irrelevant historical figure, and his followers are not second-tier artists and musicians.

Notes related to church architecture:

_____

_____

_____

_____

_____

Notes related to Jesus's influence on the visual arts:

_____

_____

_____

_____

_____

Notes related to Jesus's influence on music:

_____

_____

_____

_____

_____

Creatively uninhibited
Updated instruments
Popularly accessible

Simpler structure
Modern instruments
More creativity
Church, religious
groups, and common
citizens

Voices only
No harmonies
Church-based

Simple harmonies
Limited instruments
Music notation
Church, religious
groups, and royalty

Ancient Era

Modern Era

Medieval Era

Romantic Era

Baroque Era

Classical Era

Complex harmonies
Better instruments
Structurally clear

Renaissance Era

Increased harmonies
More instruments
Music in major and minor scales

Complex harmonies, instrumental music
Church, religious groups, royalty, and the wealthy

 **FOLLOW-UP INVESTIGATION**

Now that you've watched the video as a group, engage the following questions and discuss what you've just examined with other members of your investigative team:

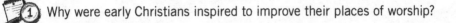 **1** Why were early Christians inspired to improve their places of worship?

_____

_____

2 Is it surprising that Christian art appeared so early within the Christian era? If so, why?

_____

_____

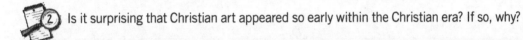 **3** **Read Isaiah 64:8.** In this verse, God is described as a "potter." Why is God described in this way? If we are created in the image of God, what does this tell us about our own creative nature?

_____

_____

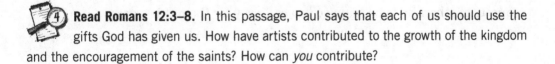 **4** **Read Romans 12:3–8.** In this passage, Paul says that each of us should use the gifts God has given us. How have artists contributed to the growth of the kingdom and the encouragement of the saints? How can *you* contribute?

_____

_____

_____

Read Exodus 35:20–29. In this passage, Moses recalls how *everyone* contributed to the artistic adornment of the tabernacle. Even if you don't think of yourself as a creative person, how can you participate creatively in the kingdom?

_____

_____

_____

_____

 The arts affect the way people think about God *and about culture.* How are Christians *currently* contributing to the arts? How can we improve our contributions? (Include Christian movies in your answer.)

_____

_____

_____

_____

Given how much data about Jesus can be recovered from the visual arts and music of the Common Era, what would it take to erase the influence of Jesus from these aspects of culture?

_____

_____

_____

_____

 # DEBRIEF, DELIBERATE, AND PRAY

Pray as a team before you close your time together. Ask God to reveal your own artistic gifts so you can help grow the kingdom in a unique way. Identify the prayer requests of others on your team so you can pray for them this week:

_____

_____

_____

_____

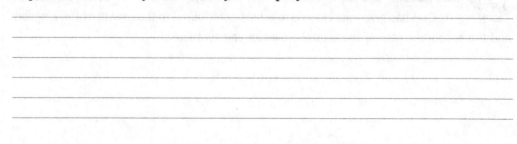

Session 7

SECONDARY INVESTIGATION

 SUMMARIZING THE EVIDENCE

Before beginning this week's secondary investigation, briefly review your surveillance video notes from session 7. In the space below, write the most significant point(s) you took away from this session.

_____

_____

_____

CONDUCTING A FORENSIC INVESTIGATION
Collecting the Evidence from Scripture

Collect the Evidence: Read Psalm 105:1–2; Colossians 3:12–17; Ephesians 5:15–21; and Revelation 14:1–3.

Examine the Facts: Music has always been a part of the Christian tradition. The earliest believers regularly sang songs, continuing a long Jewish tradition that began in antiquity. Consider, for example, the words of this worship song:

> Oh give thanks to the Lord, for he is good;
>> for his steadfast love endures forever!
>
> Let Israel say,
>> "His steadfast love endures forever."

> Let the house of Aaron say,
>> "His steadfast love endures forever."
> Let those who fear the Lord say,
>> "His steadfast love endures forever." (Psalm 118:1–4 ESV)

David first wrote these words in Psalm 118. Christians still sing these lyrics, and they have been for thousands of years. Scholars believe Psalm 118 may have been the hymn Jesus sang with his disciples at the end of the Lord's Supper (Matthew 26:30). Songs have always been an important form of Christian expression. Martin Luther described the power of music in worship: "Next to the Word of God, music deserves the highest praise. She is a mistress and governess of those human emotions. The gift of language combined with the gift of song was given to man that he should proclaim the Word of God through music."[1]

Ultimately, every one of us sings about whatever it is we worship, whether we are Christians or not. God understands that reality and calls us to worship him above all else. If we do that, we will inevitably find ourselves singing songs and using our artistic gifts to tell the world about him.

Connect the Dots: Consider the verses you've just read and take a few moments to reflect on your answers to these questions:

 Has God done any "wondrous works" (Psalm 78:4) in your life that are worthy of song?

_____

_____

_____

_____

 In Colossians 3:12–17 and Ephesians 5:15–21, Paul connects thankfulness to songs of worship. Why does Paul make this connection?

_____

_____

_____

_____

In Revelation 14, John describes our future with God. Why do you think John includes song in this description? Is song an important aspect of our life with God? If so, why?

_____

_____

_____

MAKING THE CASE
Diving Deeper into the Evidence

Review the Evidence: This section of the secondary investigation leans heavily on evidence described in *Person of Interest.* If you have the book, read chapter 7, "Jesus, the Dreary Deity?"

Make an Inference: Just as the fingerprints of Jesus can be found in the art of the earliest centuries of the Common Era, so too can they be seen in music. Hundreds of historic hymns were written in the first four centuries of the church, most *well before* Christianity was safe to sing about.

Embedded in these sacred songs were the simple truths about Jesus. The early church hymns are a rich evidential source of information about Jesus. The broad narrative of Jesus's life, ministry, death, and resurrection can be heard in these songs, along with many rich theological truths that early believers affirmed.

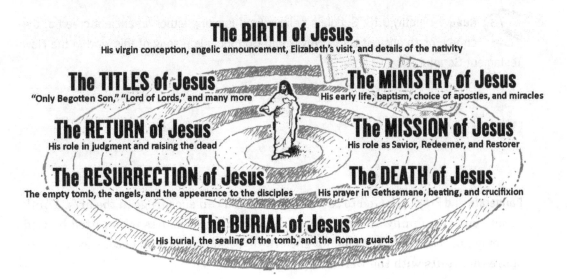

The BIRTH of Jesus
His virgin conception, angelic announcement, Elizabeth's visit, and details of the nativity

The TITLES of Jesus
"Only Begotten Son," "Lord of Lords," and many more

The MINISTRY of Jesus
His early life, baptism, choice of apostles, and miracles

The RETURN of Jesus
His role in judgment and raising the dead

The MISSION of Jesus
His role as Savior, Redeemer, and Restorer

The RESURRECTION of Jesus
The empty tomb, the angels, and the appearance to the disciples

The DEATH of Jesus
His prayer in Gethsemane, beating, and crucifixion

The BURIAL of Jesus
His burial, the sealing of the tomb, and the Roman guards

In fact, if all the New Testament manuscripts were destroyed, from Christian hymns sung in the first four centuries, we would still know the truths about Jesus mentioned in the previous graphic.

Connect the Dots: Given what you remember from the video (or what you read in the book), consider and answer the following questions:

 Why did the early Christians include so much theology in their songs and hymns?

_____

_____

_____

_____

 Read Acts 16:16–26. Given the rich theology of the early hymns, why do you think Paul and Silas were singing them, especially in this situation?

_____

_____

_____

3 Read 1 Timothy 3:16. Scholars believe Paul is citing either an ancient creed of the church or an ancient song. Why would God include a song of this kind in the New Testament Scripture?

_____

_____

_____

Deliberate and Pray: Ask God to reveal someone you can encourage in the arts. Think about your own family and friends. Is there someone who has been gifted by God but may not realize it? Ask God for specific direction so you can encourage them to share their gifts with the world.

TAKE INVESTIGATIVE NOTES

Use this page to journal and to record your reflections and notes:

Session 8

JESUS, THE ILLITERATE?

It was not by accident that the greatest thinkers
of all ages were deeply religious souls.
—MAX PLANCK

 **CASE BRIEFING**

Each year I was assigned to the detective division, I applied for advanced educational opportunities. My agency sent me to a variety of schools to help me become a better interviewer and investigator. I've always held education in high regard.

But as an atheist, I often thought of Christians as people who were *opposed* to modern education.

There weren't many Christians at my police agency, but the most outspoken one, Jason, was a blunt critic of modern education. He and his wife were unhappy with what the public schools were teaching.

Jason's conversations left a lasting impression on me as an atheist. In my view back then, Christians—if they were like Jason—were antieducation fanatics who wanted to keep their kids in the dark. Christianity appeared entirely incompatible with a proper education.

But as I continued to study the Common Era fallout, I discovered that nothing could have been further from the truth.

Jesus followers *led* the modern education revolution, and they did so because they wished to advance the values of their Master. Education is yet another form of Common Era fallout that points back to Jesus as a person of interest.

In this session, we'll investigate the impact Jesus and his followers had on modern education, from the formation of universities as we know them today to the very structure of elementary and secondary education we take for granted.

Join the rest of your team, and kick off the investigation by briefly engaging one of these questions:

- Share whether you've had an experience in school or university in which Jesus was discussed openly. What was the response from instructors or students?

  —or—

- Share a favorite memory from your school or university experience.

OPENING CLUES

Before watching the video, have someone read aloud this passage from Stephen's speech:

> At that time Moses was born, and he was no ordinary child. For three months he was cared for by his family. When he was placed outside, Pharaoh's daughter took him and brought him up as her own son. Moses was educated in all the wisdom of the Egyptians and was powerful in speech and action. (Acts 7:20–22 NIV)

Pick a second volunteer to read aloud this passage from the pen of Moses:

> This is the commandment—the statutes and the rules—that the LORD your God commanded me to teach you, that you may do them in the land to which you are going over, to possess it, that you may fear the LORD your God, you and your son and your son's son, by keeping all his statutes and his commandments, which I command you, all the days of your life, and that your days may be long. Hear therefore, O Israel, and be careful to do them, that it may go well with you, and that you may multiply greatly, as the LORD, the God of your fathers, has promised you, in a land flowing with milk and honey.
>
> Hear, O Israel: The LORD our God, the LORD is one. You shall love the LORD your God with all your heart and with all your soul and with all your might. And these words that I command you today shall be on your heart. You shall *teach them diligently to your children*, and shall talk of them when you sit in your house, and when you walk by the way, and when you lie down, and when you rise. You

shall bind them as a sign on your hand, and they shall be as frontlets between your eyes. You shall write them on the doorposts of your house and on your gates. (Deuteronomy 6:1–9 ESV, emphasis mine)

 STATEMENT ANALYSIS

Spend a few minutes reflecting on the verses you just read, then discuss these questions with your group:

How was Moses raised (according to the passage in Acts)? What did he learn as a child? How might this have set a pattern for Moses or established his own views of education?

As an adult, Moses wrote the passage from Deuteronomy. How might his own perspective as a child have affected his approach with the Israelites? When does God say education should start, and why do you think he commands this?

 SURVEILLANCE VIDEO

Play the video for session 8. As you watch, use the following section of your investigator's guide to record any thoughts or concepts that stand out to you.

Notes related to Tammy Hayes's no-body homicide case:

_____

_____

_____

_____

Notes related to how Christianity ignited an educational revolution:

Igniter #1:

_____

_____

_____

Igniter #2:

_____

_____

_____

Igniter #3:

_____

_____

_____

Igniter #4:

_____

_____

_____

Igniter #5:

_____

_____

_____

Notes related to the development of the modern university:

_____

_____

_____

_____

Notes related to the influence of Jesus followers on other forms of education:

_____

_____

_____

Notes related to reconstructing the story of Jesus from the top universities' original buildings and founding charters—their "structures" and "statements":

_____

_____

_____

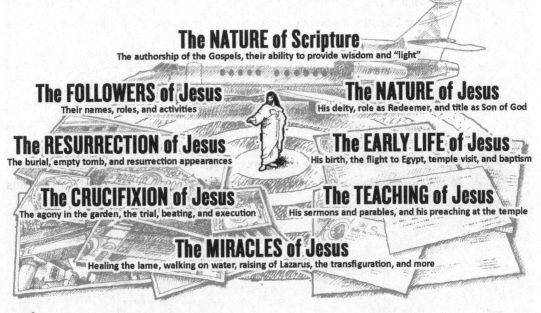

The NATURE of Scripture
The authorship of the Gospels, their ability to provide wisdom and "light"

The FOLLOWERS of Jesus
Their names, roles, and activities

The NATURE of Jesus
His deity, role as Redeemer, and title as Son of God

The RESURRECTION of Jesus
The burial, empty tomb, and resurrection appearances

The EARLY LIFE of Jesus
His birth, the flight to Egypt, temple visit, and baptism

The CRUCIFIXION of Jesus
The agony in the garden, the trial, beating, and execution

The TEACHING of Jesus
His sermons and parables, and his preaching at the temple

The MIRACLES of Jesus
Healing the lame, walking on water, raising of Lazarus, the transfiguration, and more

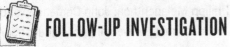

FOLLOW-UP INVESTIGATION

Now engage the following questions and discuss what you've just learned with other members of your investigative team:

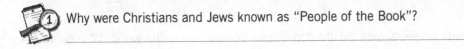

1 Why were Christians and Jews known as "People of the Book"?

_____

_____

_____

2 **Read Matthew 28:18–20 and Luke 6:40.** What does it mean to be a disciple? Does disciple-making require some form of education? If so, why? What else is included in disciple-making?

_____

_____

_____

_____

Read Romans 12:2. According to Paul, what aspect of our beings must be renewed? How have Christians advanced the cause of this kind of renewal in the history of education?

_____

_____

_____

 How would you respond to the objection that Christians have used education to colonize and advance the cause of Christianity at the expense of indigenous people groups?

_____

_____

_____

 Why do you think church leaders such as Philipp Melanchthon, John Comenius, and Jean-Baptiste de La Salle were interested in establishing universal public education?

_____

_____

_____

 Jesus followers founded the top fifteen universities in the world. Why do so few people know this fact?

_____

_____

_____

 Many universities, even though they were founded by Christians, no longer claim a Christian identity. Why is this?

_____

_____

_____

 ## DEBRIEF, DELIBERATE, AND PRAY

Ask God to impress his high regard for education on your own life. Decide what area of Bible study you are most interested in, and commit to a reading and study plan. In addition, ask God to use what you are learning in this study to heighten your own regard for education and discipleship. Identify the prayer requests of others on your team so you can pray for them this week:

Session 8

SECONDARY INVESTIGATION

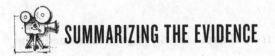

SUMMARIZING THE EVIDENCE

Before you begin this secondary investigation, take a minute to review your surveillance video notes from session 8. Use the space below to write down the most significant point(s) from this session.

_____

_____

_____

_____

_____

_____

CONDUCTING A FORENSIC INVESTIGATION
Collecting the Evidence from Scripture

Collect the Evidence: Read Proverbs 4:10–13; 22:6; Titus 1:10–16; 2:1; and 2 Timothy 2:1–2, 14–15.

Examine the Facts: The Bible authors often address young people when discussing the importance of education. While each of us must be discipled and educated by someone who is wiser than we are, we also share the responsibility of training up the next generation of Jesus followers. Everyone has this duty, even though few of us feel equipped or trained.

The goal is simple: Jesus told us to make disciples. We're called to help others learn the truth and grow in their faith so that someday they'll be able to continue the Great Commission by sharing the gospel with someone else who doesn't yet know Jesus. If we do this well, the next generation will take our place with *confidence*. As Maria Montessori, the physician and educator known for the philosophy of education that bears her name, once wrote, "The greatest sign of success for a teacher . . . is to be able to say, 'The children are now working as if I did not exist.'"[1]

The book of Proverbs is filled with encouragement for those of us who accept the Great Commission challenge, and Paul provides excellent direction to his young protégés.

Connect the Dots: Consider the evidence from Scripture you've just examined, and take a few moments to reflect on your answers to these questions:

1) Think of a bad habit you've struggled with from a young age. Why are patterns we establish early so difficult to change? Does this truth change the way you read and understand Proverbs 22:6?

_____

_____

_____

_____

_____

_____

2) Why does Paul tell Titus to "proclaim the things which are fitting for sound doctrine" (Titus 2:1)? In Titus 1:10–16, what is happening that requires Titus to make sure his teaching is sound?

_____

_____

_____

_____

_____

_____

_____

 Why does Paul tell Timothy to remember "the things which you have heard from me" (2 Timothy 2:2)? How can we make sure we each present ourselves to God "as a worker who does not need to be ashamed, accurately handling the word of truth" (2 Timothy 2:15)?

_____

_____

_____

_____

_____

MAKING THE CASE
Diving Deeper into the Evidence

Review the Evidence: This section of the secondary investigation leans heavily on evidence described in *Person of Interest*. If you have the book, read chapter 8, "Jesus, the Illiterate?"

Make an Inference: You've probably unknowingly experienced the impact of Jesus followers at some point in your education. Christians have been educational *innovators*:

Louis Braille
Education for the Blind

Frank Laubach
"Each One Teach One"

Johannes Gutenberg
Printing Press

Martin Luther
Universal Education

Thomas Hopkins Gallaudet
Education for the Deaf

Johannes Bugenhagen
School Organizer

Louis Laurent Marie Clerc
Education for the Deaf

Philipp Melanchthon
System Designer

Friedrich Froebel
Kindergarten

Charles-Michel de l'Épée
Education for the Deaf

Johann Sturm
Graded Education

Jean-Baptiste de La Salle
Compulsory Education

John Comenius
Modern Education

John Calvin
Elementary Education

Connect the Dots: Given what you remember from the video (or what you read in the book), consider the following topics and answer these questions:

 Martin Luther (1483–1546 CE), the German theologian and religious reformer, argued for universal education and literacy for children. From which passages of Scripture do you think Luther formed his passion for educating every young child?

_____

_____

_____

_____

_____

2. John Calvin (1509–1564 CE), the French theologian and reformer, promoted "a system of elementary education in the vernacular for all, including reading, writing, arithmetic, grammar, and religion."[2] Why do you think Calvin wanted to include topics *other* than religion in his educational system? How might this truth help you respond to skeptics who claim that Christians used education to subjugate people groups?

_____

_____

_____

3. Friedrich Froebel (1782–1852 CE), the son of a Lutheran pastor, is known as the "father of kindergarten education." Why is early education important? Which Bible verses address this important topic?

_____

_____

_____

_____

Deliberate and Pray: Ask God to help you identify someone you can learn from and someone you can teach. Ask him to increase your own understanding of the power and responsibility of discipleship, and ask that he move you to *act*.

TAKE INVESTIGATIVE NOTES

Use this page to journal and to record your reflections and notes:

OBJECTION: CHRISTIANITY ADVOCATES VIOLENCE TO ADVANCE THE GOSPEL

Skeptics sometimes claim Christians haven't historically advanced the gospel with a well-reasoned, educated approach, but have instead acted violently to force people to convert to Christianity. Have people behaved violently under the Christian banner? Yes. Does the *Christian worldview as taught by Jesus* endorse this approach? No. Christianity grew exponentially in the earliest centuries of the Common Era, when followers of Jesus were powerless, persecuted, and pursued. They simply obeyed the counterintuitive commands of their Master to love their enemies (Matthew 5:44), turn the other cheek (Matthew 5:39), and to pray for those who abused them (Luke 6:28). Christianity grew not as a result of violence, but as Christ followers advanced education across the globe.

Session 9

JESUS, THE SCIENCE DENIER?

A scientific discovery is also a religious discovery.
There is no conflict between science and religion.
Our knowledge of God is made larger with every
discovery we make about the world.
—JOSEPH H. TAYLOR JR.

 **CASE BRIEFING**

Detectives solve cases every day using forensic evidence. DNA technology, chemical or material comparisons, and other contemporary scientific processes aid detectives as they investigate and solve cold cases.

Unfortunately, not many of my cases benefited from these forensic disciplines.

Even though technology improved over the years, my cases were unusual. They typically lacked the type of evidence that could be examined scientifically. I did my best to employ the forensic technology whenever possible, however, because I'm not opposed to using science to determine the truth.

But my Christian coworker, Jason, seemed to hold a *different* view.

When he told me about his frustration with his kids' schools, he focused on one aspect of public education that he and his wife found particularly objectionable: the theory of evolution. He rejected the hypothesis and opposed the way it was taught in the public schools in his area.

"They teach it as though it's a fact, when it's just a theory," he said.

"Do you also reject the theory of gravity?" I asked.

As an atheist, I couldn't believe that Christians still rejected what I considered to be established science. Christianity seemed incompatible with scientific discovery, and Christians seemed entirely unwilling to abandon their irrational belief in the supernatural.

I suspected that *all* Christians held a view like my friend Jason, resisting the advances of science as though every new scientific discovery put another nail in God's coffin. Back then I believed there were already many nails in that casket. I expected science would someday solve all the questions once answered by primitive theologians—*if* stubborn Christians like Jason would just stop opposing science at every turn. I resonated with the statement of Catherine Fahringer, a social activist and officer at the Freedom from Religion Foundation, who once said, "We would be 1,500 years ahead if it hadn't been for the church dragging science back by its coattails and burning our best minds at the stake."[1]

In this session, we'll examine the relationship between Christian belief and the advancement of the sciences. Have Jesus followers been anti-science? Or is it possible that they *led* the sciences because of the worldview they learned from their Master? We'll discover the answer in this week's investigation. Before you begin as a group, engage one of these topics:

- Share whether you've had an experience with someone who believes in Jesus but is skeptical of science.

    —or—

- Share what you believe about the relationship between science and religious belief.

OPENING CLUES

Before watching the video, ask someone in your group to read this Psalm aloud:

> Praise the LORD!
> I will give thanks to the LORD with all my heart,
> In the company of the upright and in the assembly.
> Great are the works of the LORD;
> They are studied by all who delight in them.
> Splendid and majestic is His work,
> And His righteousness endures forever. (Psalm 111:1–3)

Next ask someone in your group to read this verse:

By faith we understand that the world has been created by the word of God so that what is seen has not been made out of things that are visible. (Hebrews 11:3)

Finally, ask someone in your group to read aloud how Paul describes Jesus:

He is the image of the invisible God, the firstborn of all creation: for by Him all things were created, both in the heavens and on earth, visible and invisible, whether thrones, or dominions, or rulers, or authorities—all things have been created through Him and for Him. He is before all things, and in Him all things hold together. (Colossians 1:15–17)

STATEMENT ANALYSIS

Spend a few minutes reflecting on the verses you just read, then discuss these questions with your group:

What does the psalmist encourage us to do in relationship to God's great works? Might verses like these encourage believers to examine the creation of God?

How does the writer of Hebrews describe the relationship between the visible world and invisible forces?

How does Paul identify Jesus?

Why might passages like these in the New Testament further encourage Jesus followers to examine their environment?

SURVEILLANCE VIDEO

Play the video for session 9. As you watch, use the following section of your investigator's guide to record any thoughts or concepts that stand out to you.

OBJECTION: CHRISTIANITY IS ANTI-SCIENCE

Christianity isn't anti-science, but it is anti-scientism. Scientism is the belief that science is the only way to know anything. But there are many things we know without the benefit of science at all, like logical and mathematical truths (which precede scientific investigations), metaphysical truths (which determine if the external world is real), moral and ethical truths (which set boundaries for our behavior), aesthetic truths (like determining beauty), and historical truths. Christians believe that science can tell us many important things but not *all* of the important things.

Notes related to Tammy Hayes's no-body homicide case:

_____

_____

_____

Notes related to Galileo:

_____

_____

_____

Notes related to the progress of science:

_____

_____

_____

Notes related to Christianity's impact on science:

Igniter #1:

_____

_____

Igniter #2:

_____

_____

Igniter #3:

_____

_____

Igniter #4:

_____

_____

Igniter #5:

_____

_____

Igniter #6:

_____

_____

Igniter #7:

_____

_____

Notes related to the science "hall of fame":

_____

_____

_____

_____

Notes related to the "science fathers" and award winners:

_____

_____

_____

_____

_____

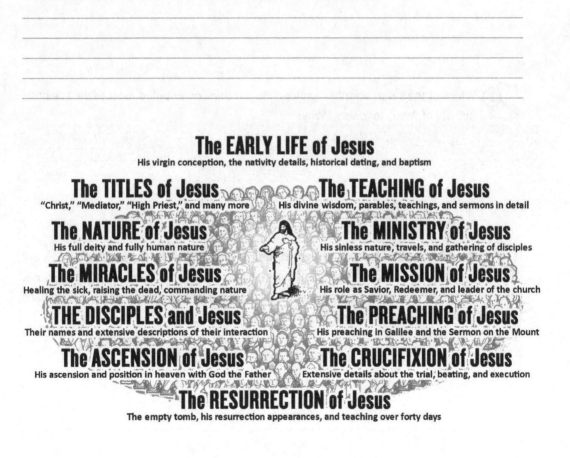

The EARLY LIFE of Jesus
His virgin conception, the nativity details, historical dating, and baptism

The TITLES of Jesus
"Christ," "Mediator," "High Priest," and many more

The TEACHING of Jesus
His divine wisdom, parables, teachings, and sermons in detail

The NATURE of Jesus
His full deity and fully human nature

The MINISTRY of Jesus
His sinless nature, travels, and gathering of disciples

The MIRACLES of Jesus
Healing the sick, raising the dead, commanding nature

The MISSION of Jesus
His role as Savior, Redeemer, and leader of the church

THE DISCIPLES and Jesus
Their names and extensive descriptions of their interaction

The PREACHING of Jesus
His preaching in Galilee and the Sermon on the Mount

The ASCENSION of Jesus
His ascension and position in heaven with God the Father

The CRUCIFIXION of Jesus
Extensive details about the trial, beating, and execution

The RESURRECTION of Jesus
The empty tomb, his resurrection appearances, and teaching over forty days

Notes related to reconstructing the Jesus story from the science fathers:

_____

_____

_____

 **FOLLOW-UP INVESTIGATION**

Now that you've watched the video as a group, engage the following questions and discuss what you've just examined with other members of your investigative team:

 Why do many people return to the story of Galileo to demonstrate that Jesus and his followers were "anti-science"?

_____

_____

_____

_____

 Which of the seven science "igniters" do you think contributed most to the scientific activity of Jesus followers? Why?

_____

_____

_____

_____

 Read Psalm 19:1–4. David wrote that the "heavens tell of the glory of God" (v. 1), but he also said they don't use speech or words to tell us about God. If this is the case, how can the heavens tell us anything about God? How might scientists who are Christians use this passage to motivate them in their studies?

_____

_____

_____

_____

Read Romans 1:18–20. Paul wrote that all of us—even those who deny God's existence or role in creation—ought to know that God exists. How does Paul say this should be evident? Paul says God's "eternal power and divine nature" (v. 20) can be known from "what has been made" (v. 20). Once again, how might scientists who believe in Jesus use this verse as motivation in their studies?

_____

_____

_____

Read Isaiah 40:12. Isaiah describes God's knowledge and power over the physical world in an interesting way in this passage. How might this have motivated Jesus followers to study the physical realm?

_____

_____

_____

Why is our ability to reconstruct the story of Jesus from the personal writings of history's foremost scientists particularly powerful?

_____

_____

_____

What might you now say (given what you've learned about the Jesus-following "science fathers") to someone who says, "I only trust what scientists say"?

_____

_____

_____

_____

DEBRIEF, DELIBERATE, AND PRAY

Ask God to give you confidence and the courage to tell others about the true relationship between Christianity and science. Ask him to help you identify a young, budding Jesus follower who is interested in the sciences so you can encourage him or her to continue their studies for the glory of God. Identify the prayer requests of others on your team so you can pray for them this week:

Session 9

SECONDARY INVESTIGATION

 SUMMARIZING THE EVIDENCE

Before you begin this secondary investigation, briefly review your surveillance video notes from session 9. In the space below, write the most significant point(s) you took away from this session.

_____

_____

_____

 CONDUCTING A FORENSIC INVESTIGATION
Collecting the Evidence from Scripture

Collect the Evidence: Read Genesis 1:10–13; Nehemiah 9:5–6; Job 9:8–10; and Luke 12:22–27.

Examine the Facts: Christ followers have initiated, elevated, or perfected every major field of scientific study. Jesus followers didn't simply contribute to the sciences, they *founded* and *led* them. That's why many Jesus-following scientists have been award winners. Christians have claimed the world's most prestigious scientific awards, winning medals and prizes from over one hundred scientific institutions, societies, academies, associations, and universities.

Many of these award-winning men and women—in an incredibly diverse range of scientific disciplines—considered their scientific contributions a holy investigation into the mind of the Creator and the highest act of devotion to God. Physicist

Ernest Walton, the 1951 Nobel Prize winner in physics who was the first person in history to split the atom, put it this way: "One way to learn the mind of the Creator is to study His creation. We must pay God the compliment of studying His work of art and this should apply to all realms of human thought. A refusal to use our intelligence honestly is an act of contempt for Him who gave us that intelligence."[1]

The Old and New Testaments provide clues as to why Christians have explored many diverse scientific disciplines with an attitude similar to that of Ernest Walton.

Connect the Dots: Consider what you've just examined and take a few moments to reflect on your answers to these questions:

1. Looking at the creative activity of God in the Genesis passage, list which areas of scientific exploration Jesus followers might engage in to learn more about God. What aspect of God's creation described in this passage inspires you most as evidence for his existence and power?

_____

_____

_____

2. What aspect of God's creation do Nehemiah and Job describe? What scientific disciplines encompass the study of this facet of God's creative activity? What do you think we can learn about God's power or nature from this field of study?

_____

_____

_____

3. Luke demonstrates God's concern for detail in his creation. How many aspects of God's creation does Jesus describe in this passage? Jesus is trying to make a point about our dependence on God. How might the study of science increase our trust in God?

_____

_____

_____

 **MAKING THE CASE**
Diving Deeper into the Evidence

Review the Evidence: As in other sessions, this part of the secondary investigation leans heavily on evidence described in *Person of Interest*. If you have the book, read chapter 9, "Jesus, the Science Denier?"

Make an Inference: In a 2019 poll, Americans were asked about their level of trust in a variety of institutions and experts. Scientists topped the list of trusted authorities, ahead of the military, police officers, public school officials, religious leaders, university professors, journalists, business leaders, and politicians (in that order).[2] If a scientist says it, most people are inclined to believe it.

Most people *expect* the primitive theologians and church fathers to have something to say about Jesus, but they don't trust their authority. Instead, they trust scientists, whom they assume have nothing to do with or say about Jesus.

But as this session has demonstrated, the nearly one thousand premier, Christ-following scientists described in *Person of Interest* also had something to say about Jesus. Many of them wrote extensively about their faith and the man they believed was the Son of God. In every significant claim related to Jesus, the science fathers agree with the church fathers.

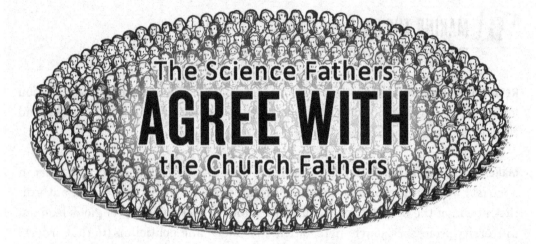

That's right, men and women who founded the disciplines of physics and chemistry, biology and cosmology, evolutionary genetics and quantum mechanics *also* believed that Jesus performed miracles and rose from the grave. They were certain that the supernatural author of the laws they studied had the power to intervene in the natural world and that he had done so in the person of interest known as Jesus of Nazareth.

Connect the Dots: Given what you remember from the video (or what you read in the book), consider and answer the following questions:

 Why do many people see Christianity and science as incompatible? How might you communicate what you've learned in this session to others?

_____

_____

_____

_____

Johannes Kepler (the German mathematician, astronomer, and theologian who was a key figure in the scientific revolution) once wrote, "I was merely thinking God's thoughts after him. Since we astronomers are priests of the highest God in regard to the book of nature, it benefits us to be thoughtful, not of the glory of our minds, but rather, above all else, of the glory of God."[3] What do you think Kepler meant when he said he "was merely thinking God's thoughts after him"? What do you think he meant by calling the natural world the "book of nature"?

_____

_____

_____

_____

 Why might it be particularly important to communicate to unbelievers that the science fathers saw no conflict between their study of science and their belief in Jesus's miracles and resurrection?

_____

_____

_____

_____

Deliberate and Pray: Ask God to increase your awareness and interest in the sciences. Ask him to guide you to additional resources that can help you think and speak persuasively about the sciences.

TAKE INVESTIGATIVE NOTES

Use this page to journal and to record your reflections and notes:

_____

_____

_____

_____

_____

_____

_____

_____

_____

_____

_____

JESUS, THE ONE AND ONLY?

In Jesus Christ, the reality of God entered into the reality of
this world. . . . Henceforth one can speak neither of God nor
of the world without speaking of Jesus Christ. All concepts of
reality which do not take account of Him are abstractions.

—DIETRICH BONHOEFFER

 **CASE BRIEFING**

"Do you ever wonder if all this would have been different if we were living someplace else?" asked Susie, pointing to the tall stack of research books piled up in the corner of our bedroom.

"What do you mean?"

"Well, if we had been raised in a Muslim country, would you be investigating Islam?"

"Maybe," I replied. "But even if we had been raised in a Muslim country, we still would have learned a lot about Jesus . . ."

I was surprised to discover yet another way Jesus affected the fallout of the Common Era, and this line of evidence involved groups, like Muslims, who don't include the New Testament in their collection of holy writings.

After the inauguration of Christianity, ancient religions—along with the religions that *followed* Christianity in history—found themselves contending with Jesus's overwhelming impact. Some responded by *modifying* their practices and beliefs to mimic Christianity, some simply *mentioned* Jesus, and others found a way to *merge* him into their worldview.

Jesus *matters* even to followers of other religions.

Why would this be the case, especially since Jesus claimed to be the *exclusive* path to God? Jesus never modified, merged, or mentioned other faith systems, religious leaders, or deities, even though these systems found a place for Jesus within their teaching.

We'll examine this unique truth in this week's session as we discover why Jesus matters in every important aspect of the Common Era fallout. We'll also explore why Jesus ought to matter to us and to everyone we know.

Before we jump in, take some time with your group to address one of these topics:

- Share an experience you had trying to tell a member of a different faith system about Jesus.

  —or—

- Share an experience in which someone of a different religion tried to share what they believed with *you*.

OPENING CLUES

Before you start watching this week's video, pick a volunteer to read aloud from this Scripture written by Jeremiah:

Now Ahab the son of Omri became king over Israel in the thirty-eighth year of Asa king of Judah, and Ahab the son of Omri reigned over Israel in Samaria for twenty-two years. Ahab the son of Omri did evil in the sight of the LORD more than all who were before him.

And as though it had been a trivial thing for him to walk in the sins of Jeroboam the son of Nebat, he married Jezebel the daughter of Ethbaal king of the Sidonians, and went and served Baal, and worshiped him. So he erected an altar for Baal at the house of Baal, which he built in Samaria. Ahab also made the Asherah. So Ahab did more to provoke the LORD God of Israel to anger than all the kings of Israel who were before him. (1 Kings 16:29–33)

Next, read aloud this passage, written by the apostle Paul:

Now about food sacrificed to idols: We know that "We all possess knowledge." But knowledge puffs up while love builds up. Those who think they know something do not yet know as they ought to know. But whoever loves God is known by God.

So then, about eating food sacrificed to idols: We know that "An idol is nothing at all in the world" and that "There is no God but one." For even if there are so-called gods, whether in heaven or on earth (as indeed there are many "gods" and many "lords"), yet for us there is but one God, the Father, from whom all things came and for whom we live; and there is but one Lord, Jesus Christ, through whom all things came and through whom we live. (1 Corinthians 8:1–6 NIV)

STATEMENT ANALYSIS

Spend a few minutes reflecting on the verses you just read, then discuss these questions with your group:

Why did Jeremiah write that Ahab "did more to provoke the LORD God of Israel to anger than all the kings of Israel who were before him" (1 Kings 16:33)?

The Israelites were clearly aware of all the ancient deities and mythologies that surrounded them. Why was God so adamant about preventing other forms of worship from influencing the worship of the one true God? How do you think God would have responded to any modification of Judaism because of the influence of these competing religious systems?

Paul was also aware of the contemporary idols and competing religious claims of his time. How did he describe these gods compared with Jesus?

SURVEILLANCE VIDEO

Play the video for session 10. This surveillance video, like session 1, is slightly longer than the others. As you watch, use the following section of your investigator's guide to record any thoughts or concepts that stand out to you.

OBJECTION: ALL GOD EXPECTS OF US IS SINCERITY

Is sincerity more important to God than accuracy? Imagine that you and I are hiking and discover a poisonous hemlock plant. Since it looks like parsley, you decide to eat some of it. You sincerely believe the plant is parsley. Will your sincerity protect you from harm? Most of us understand the value of truth and sincerity. Both are important, but sincerity without truth can lead you to the wrong place and endanger your life.

Notes related to Tammy Hayes's no-body homicide case:

_____

_____

_____

_____

_____

_____

_____

Notes related to Jesus's impact on ancient religions:

Hinduism:

_____

_____

_____

_____

Notes related to Jesus's impact on modern religions:

Buddhism:

_____

_____

_____

_____

Islam:

_____

_____

_____

_____

Bahá'í:

_____

_____

_____

_____

Islamic Ahmadiyya movement:

_____

_____

_____

_____

Notes related to what can be known about Jesus from other religious systems:

_____

_____

_____

_____

_____

Mirza Ghulam
Ahmad
(Ahmadiyya)

Deepak Chopra
(New

Indra

The CHILDHOOD of Jesus
His virgin conception, the announcement of the star, and the nativity scene

Bahá'u
(Bahá

The TITLES of Jesus
"Son of God," "Lord," and "Messiah"

The MINISTRY of Jesus
His sinless nature, baptism by John, and his miracles

The RETURN of Jesus
His role in the final judgment and his return

The TEACHING of Jesus
His sermons, parables, teaching, and transfiguration

The DISCIPLES of Jesus
The twelve apostles, Peter's prominence, and Lord's Supper

The CRUCIFIXION of Jesus
The trial, crucifixion, death, and purpose

The RESURRECTION of Jesus
The appearance to the disciples and the ascension

Muhammad
(Islam)

Buddha
(Buddhism)

Mithras

Krishna

Notes related to the unlikely impact of Jesus:

_____

_____

_____

_____

_____

Notes related to the conclusion of Tammy Hayes's no-body homicide case:

_____

_____

_____

_____

_____

_____

_____

_____

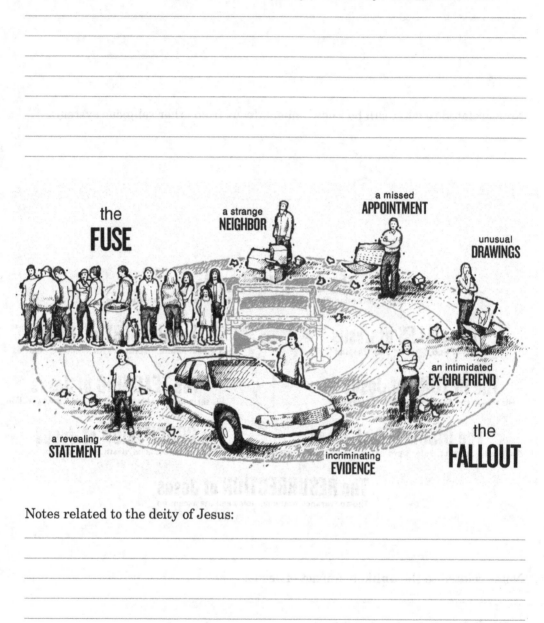

Notes related to the deity of Jesus:

_____

_____

_____

_____

_____

_____

_____

Notes related to why Jesus matters:

_____

_____

_____

_____

_____

FOLLOW-UP INVESTIGATION

Now that you've watched the last video as a group, engage the following questions and discuss what you've just examined with other members of your investigative team:

1. Why do other religious systems (even those that began *prior* to Jesus's arrival), find it necessary to mention him, merge him into their worldview, or modify their claims to include him?

_____

_____

_____

_____

Which non-Christian religious system do you think accommodates Jesus most robustly? Why do you think Jesus influenced this religion more than the others?

_____

_____

_____

_____

 Read John 14:1–11. How accommodating was Jesus (in verse 6) when referencing alternative paths to God? Look at verses 9–11, and list the basis for Jesus's claim in verse 6.

_____

_____

_____

_____

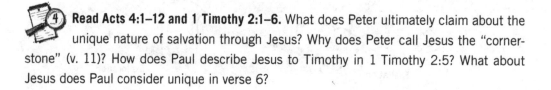 **Read Acts 4:1–12 and 1 Timothy 2:1–6.** What does Peter ultimately claim about the unique nature of salvation through Jesus? Why does Peter call Jesus the "cornerstone" (v. 11)? How does Paul describe Jesus to Timothy in 1 Timothy 2:5? What about Jesus does Paul consider unique in verse 6?

_____

_____

_____

_____

Peter and Paul simply affirm the teaching of Jesus related to his exclusive ability to bring people to the Father. If someone asked you why Jesus was the only way to God, how would you respond?

_____

_____

_____

_____

Now that you've finished examining the many ways Jesus has affected the Common Era fallout, which of these areas of influence was most surprising? Why?

_____

_____

_____

 If someone asked you to summarize why Jesus matters, what would you say? If someone asked you to defend the deity of Jesus, what would you say?

_____

_____

_____

_____

 ## DEBRIEF, DELIBERATE, AND PRAY

Ask God to bless the efforts of everyone on your investigative team as this study concludes. Ask God to provide opportunities for each of you to share what you've learned. Make a list of the final prayer requests for members of your team:

_____

_____

_____

_____

_____

_____

_____

_____

_____

_____

_____

Session 10

SECONDARY INVESTIGATION

 ## SUMMARIZING THE EVIDENCE

Before you begin this final secondary investigation, briefly review your surveillance video notes from session 10. In the space below, write the most significant point(s) you recall from this session.

_____

_____

_____

CONDUCTING A FORENSIC INVESTIGATION
Collecting the Evidence from Scripture

Collect the Evidence: Read John 5:25; 8:23–24; 8:49–59; 10:25–33; 18:36–37; and Matthew 13:41.

Examine the Facts: The evidence from the fuse and the fallout exposes two important truths: First, *no* person has had the kind of impact Jesus had on history. Second, every reconstruction of the Jesus story from the literature, art, music, education, and science fallout describes Jesus as *God incarnate.*

Is that true? Is it possible that Jesus was something more than a man? Do the gospel eyewitness accounts provide some context and explain why the explosive appearance of Jesus inaugurated the Common Era? That's the question that caused me, as an atheist, to suspend my skepticism of the Bible just long enough to investigate the Gospels.

I began by *testing* them.

Were these ancient documents penned early enough to have been written (or sourced) by true eyewitnesses? Could they be corroborated in some way? Were the authors honest and accurate over time? Did the writers possess a bias that would cause them to lie? I evaluated the Gospels using this same four-part template I used to assess eyewitnesses in criminal trials. In the end, the Gospels passed this reliability test, adding additional evidence to explain why Jesus—the unlikeliest of suspects—inaugurated the Common Era (much more, of course, could be said about this aspect of my investigation, but that's the topic of my first book, *Cold-Case Christianity*).

The Gospels—the eyewitness accounts of ancient Jesus followers—helped me to understand why the appearance of Jesus changed our calendar and inspired the world.

Connect the Dots: Consider the verses you just read and take a few moments to reflect on your answers to these questions:

 How does Jesus begin his statement in John 5:25? How is this different from how the prophets of the Old Testament began their proclamations (Isaiah 10:24, for example)? Does this difference demonstrate that Jesus viewed himself as God? If so, how?

_____

_____

_____

_____

 How does Jesus describe where he came from in John 8:23–24 and John 18:36–37? Do these statements by Jesus lend support to the claim that Jesus referred to himself as God? If so, how?

_____

_____

_____

_____

 To whom did Jesus say the angels belonged in Matthew 13:41? Why might this claim also support his view of himself as God?

_____

_____

_____

In John 8:49–59, the Pharisees questioned Jesus's power, authority, and teaching. What did Jesus mean when he said, "Before Abraham was born, I am!" (v. 58)? How did the Pharisees' response in verse 59 demonstrate that they understood Jesus was claiming to be God?

_____

_____

_____

In John 10:25–33, Jesus refers to his miracles when making a case for his deity. What did Jesus mean when he said, "I and the Father are one" (v. 30)? How did the Jews interpret this claim (in verse 33)? Why did Jesus claim that the miracles he worked proved he was God (in verse 32)?

_____

_____

_____

_____

MAKING THE CASE
Diving Deeper into the Evidence

Review the Evidence: This part of the secondary investigation leans heavily on evidence described in *Person of Interest*. If you have the book, read chapter 10, "Jesus, the One and Only?," and the postscript, "The Unlikeliest of Suspects."

Make an Inference: "I'm hearing this verse in a different way now . . ." Susie had just finished reading the Gospels and recalled an oft-quoted verse from the gospel of John: "Jesus said, 'No one comes to the Father except through me.'"

"How does it seem different?" I asked. Susie knew I had been researching how other religions perceived Jesus, and I had been updating her along the way.

"Jesus doesn't make room for other religions, other gods, or other . . . *paths*. He doesn't accommodate them in any way. He never even *refers* to them."

Susie's observation was strikingly true. While the person of Jesus impressed the leaders of other religious worldviews, the gods, goddesses, prophets, mystics, and religious leaders of these faith systems failed to impress Jesus. Many of these world religions preceded Christianity, yet none of the New Testament writers mentioned their names or merged their claims.

In the years since Christianity was established, many other world religions have emerged. While these worldviews all acknowledged Jesus in some way, Christianity didn't modify its claims to embrace their prophets, "manifestations," or deities.

The religions of the world made room for Jesus, but Jesus never budged. His teaching mattered to the other religions, but Krishna, the Buddha, Muhammad, Bahá'u'lláh, and Ahmad *combined* didn't have a similar impact on Christianity. *That*, I thought, was remarkable.

"Maybe it's because the other religions aren't true," said Susie after a long pause.

And there it was: the relationship between what's *true* and what *matters*.

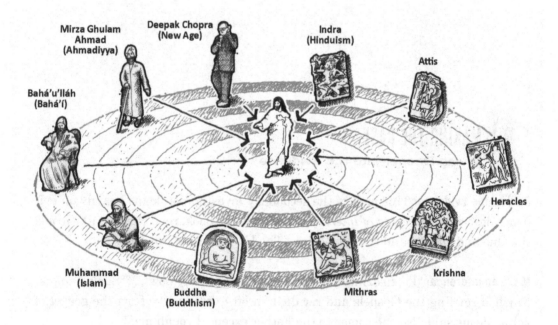

Connect the Dots: Given what you remember from the video (or what you read in the book), consider and answer the following questions:

1 What aspect of the Common Era fallout (as described in this investigation) has been most important to you personally? How has Jesus shaped this facet of human history?

_____

_____

_____

_____

2 Does truth influence what matters to you? If so, why? Can you imagine a scenario in which something untrue would shape the way you live your life? Describe a time when something untrue occupied your thoughts. Is it important that Christianity is *true* as well as historically *influential*? If so, why?

_____

_____

_____

_____

3 Does the deity of Jesus matter? If so, why? If you believe Jesus is the Son of God, does this truth change the way you think about Jesus? If so, how?

_____

_____

_____

_____

_____

Deliberate and Pray: As you reach the conclusion of this investigation, ask God to help you grow in your confidence as a result of this study. Ask him to help you communicate the truth about Jesus to others. Ask him to help you rely on this truth, even when you encounter hardship and crisis.

OBJECTION: IT'S NARROW-MINDED TO THINK JESUS IS THE ONLY WAY TO GOD

Christians don't claim Jesus is the only way to God. *Jesus* claimed he was the only way to God. He said, "I am the way and the truth and the life. No one comes to the Father except through me" (John 14:6 NIV). That's an exclusive claim, but what if it's true? Doctors claim isoniazid is the only cure for tuberculosis. That's also an exclusive claim. Are they being narrow-minded? What if their claim is simply true? Isn't it more important to investigate the claim than to dismiss it out of hand because you think it's narrow-minded?

 TAKE INVESTIGATIVE NOTES

Use this page to journal and to record your reflections and notes:

CLOSING DISPATCH FROM J. WARNER

No one else holds or has held the place in the heart of the
world which Jesus holds. Other gods have been as devoutly
worshipped; no other man has been so devoutly loved.
—JOHN KNOX

Congratulations for your involvement in this investigation of Jesus as a person of interest. If you completed all ten sessions, you know how the fuse and fallout of human history points *uniquely* to Jesus of Nazareth.

History predicted his coming and aligned itself in preparation. Worshipers imagined and readied themselves before he was born. Governments laid the foundation for his arrival. No other singular person—*in all of history*—matched the prophecies, fulfilled the expectations, and leveraged human events as did Jesus.

After his arrival, Jesus changed the trajectory of literature, art, music, education, science, and religion. He established the worldview that inaugurated the Common Era and gave birth to the disciplines that make humans . . . *human*.

Jesus mattered then, and he still matters today.

If you finished this investigative series, you also know how unlikely it is that someone like Jesus (given his social status, economic position, and geographic birthplace) would be capable of such unparalleled impact and transformation. *No one* changed the world like Jesus, and he left his fingerprints so clearly on human history that his story can be completely reconstructed *even without the New Testament*.

Only God incarnate could have that kind of impact and leave that kind of evidence trail.

Now that you're finished investigating, it's time to make your case to a jury. All of us know someone who is unfamiliar with the historical "explosion" known as

Jesus. Now is the time to share what you've learned. Make the case from the fuse and the fallout. Tell others why Jesus matters.

We also know people who are skeptical of the Bible and doubt the reliability of the New Testament gospels. Let's help them understand that Jesus left more historical fallout than anyone else in history. Let's show them how to reconstruct the story of Jesus from the rubble.

I've never conducted a successful investigation that I didn't enthusiastically present to a district attorney and then to a jury. Now it's *your* turn to present what you've learned. Help others to understand how God came into his creation and changed everything. Demonstrate—from the evidence—that Jesus is history's most important person of interest.

J. Warner Wallace

LEAD INVESTIGATOR'S GUIDE

If you are reading this, you have likely agreed to lead a group through this *Person of Interest Investigator's Guide*. Thank you! What you have chosen to do is important, and much good fruit can come from the investigation you are about to guide. The rewards of being a lead investigator are different from those of the other investigators in your group, and I am confident you will be encouraged and equipped as you lead others through the evidence.

This ten-session investigation has been constructed around video content and small-group interaction. As the lead investigator, imagine yourself as a seasoned detective facilitating a team of young investigators. Your job is to take care of your trainees by managing all the behind-the-scenes details so that as your investigators arrive, they can interact with one another and examine the evidence together.

As the lead investigator, you do not need to answer all the questions or reteach the content—the videos, book, and investigator's guide will do most of that work. Your job is to guide the experience, cultivate your team, and facilitate the learning experience. Create a place where members can process, question, and reflect—not receive more instruction.

Several elements in this lead investigator's guide will help you structure your study and reflection time, so follow along and take advantage of each one.

BEFORE YOU BEGIN

Before your first meeting, make sure the other investigators each have a copy of the investigator's guide so they have time to look over the material and can ask any preliminary questions. Alternately, you can hand out the investigator's guides at your first meeting. During your first meeting, be sure to record the names, phone numbers, and email addresses of your team so you can keep in touch with them during the week.

The ideal size for an investigative group is eight to ten people, which ensures that everyone will have a chance to participate in discussions. If you have more people, you might want to break up into subgroups after watching the video. Encourage those who show up at the first meeting to commit to attending the duration of the study, as this will help the group members get to know one another, create stability for the group, and help you know how to prepare each week.

Each of the sessions begins with a "Case Briefing" to introduce the session. The "Opening Clues" will provide you with topics and questions that can serve as an icebreaker to get the group members thinking about the topic at hand. Some people may want to tell a long story in response to one of these questions or "clues," but the goal is to keep the answers brief. Ideally, you want everyone in the group to have a chance to answer, so try to keep the responses to a minute or less. Give each member of the investigative team a chance to answer, but tell them to feel free to pass if they wish.

With the rest of the investigation, it's generally not a good idea to have everyone answer every question—a free-flowing discussion is more desirable. But with the opening icebreaker questions, you can go around the circle. Encourage shy people to share, but don't force them.

Let the group members know that each session contains a secondary investigation: five days' worth of Bible study and reflection materials they can complete during the week. While this is an optional opportunity, it will help the members cement the concepts presented during the group study time and encourage them to spend time each day in God's Word. Also invite them to bring any questions and insights they uncovered during the week to your next meeting, especially if they had a breakthrough moment or if they didn't understand something.

WEEKLY PREPARATION

As the lead investigator, you should do a few things to prepare for each meeting:

- Read through the session. This will help you to become familiar with the content and know how to structure the discussion times.

- Decide which questions you definitely want to discuss. Depending on the length of your group discussion, you may not get through all the "surveillance video" and "follow-up investigation" questions, so choose four to five that you want to be sure to cover.
- Be familiar with the questions you want to discuss. When the group meets, you'll be watching the clock, so you want to make sure you are familiar with the questions you have selected. In this way, you'll ensure you have the material deeply ingrained in your mind.
- Pray for your team. Pray for your group members throughout the week, and ask God to lead them as they study his Word.
- Bring extra supplies to your meeting. The individual investigators should bring their own pens for writing notes, but it's a good idea to have extras available for those who forget. You may also want to bring paper and additional Bibles.

Note that in many cases there will be no one "right" answer to a question. Answers will vary, especially when the group members are being asked to share their personal experiences.

STRUCTURING THE DISCUSSION TIME

You will need to determine (along with your investigative team) how long you want to meet each week so you can plan your time accordingly. Generally, most groups like to meet for either sixty minutes or ninety minutes, so you could use one of the following schedules:

SECTION	60 MINUTES	120 MINUTES
Case Briefing (members arrive and get settled)	5 minutes	15 minutes
Opening Clues / Statement Analysis (discuss one of the two opening questions)	10 minutes	25 minutes
Surveillance Video (watch the teaching material together and take notes)	10–15+ minutes	10–15+ minutes
Follow-Up Investigation (discuss the Bible study questions you selected ahead of time)	25 minutes	60 minutes
Debrief, Deliberate, and Pray (pray together as a group and dismiss)	5 minutes	10 minutes

As the lead investigator, you need to keep track of time and keep things moving along according to your schedule. You might want to set a timer for each segment so both you and the group members know when time is up. Keep in mind that the videos for sessions 1 and 10 are considerably longer than those of sessions 2 through 8. Be sure to allow yourself extra time.

Don't be concerned if the group members are quiet or slow to share. People are often quiet when they are pulling together their ideas, and this might be a new experience for them. Just ask a question and let it hang in the air until someone shares. You can then say, "Thank you. What about others? What came to you when you watched that portion of the video?"

GROUP DYNAMICS

Leading a team of investigators through the *Person of Interest Investigator's Guide* will prove to be highly rewarding both to you and your group. But this doesn't mean you will not encounter challenges along the way! Discussions can get off track. Team members may not be sensitive to the needs and ideas of others. Some might worry they will be expected to talk about matters that make them feel awkward. Others may express comments that result in disagreements. To help ease this strain on you and the team, consider the following ground rules:

- When someone raises a question or comment that is off the main topic, suggest you deal with it another time, or, if you feel led to go in that direction, let the group know you will spend some time discussing it.
- At your discretion, feel free to invite specific team members to comment on questions that call for personal experience.
- If you find one or two people are dominating the discussion time, direct a few questions to others on the team. Outside the main group time, ask the dominating members to help you draw out the quieter ones. Work to make them a part of the solution instead of the problem.
- When a disagreement occurs, encourage the team members to process the matter in love. Encourage those on opposite sides to restate what they heard the other side say about the matter, and then invite each side to evaluate if that perception is accurate. Lead the investigative team in examining other Bible passages related to the topic, and look for common ground.

When any of these issues arise, encourage your team members to follow these words from the Bible: "Love one another" (John 13:34), "If it is possible, as far as it depends on you, live at peace with everyone" (Romans 12:18 NIV), and "Be quick to listen, slow to speak and slow to become angry" (James 1:19 NIV). This will make your time together more rewarding and beneficial for everyone who attends.

NOTES

Session 1: Secondary Investigation

1. Richard Dawkins, "Has the World Changed?," *The Guardian*, October 11, 2001.

Session 2: Jesus, the Average Ancient?

1. Dictionary.com, s.v. "opportunity," accessed March 27, 2021, https://www.dictionary.com/browse/opportunity.

Session 2: Secondary Investigation

1. Martin Luther, *Martin Luther: Selections from His Writings,* ed. John Dillenberger (New York: Anchor, 1962), 18.
2. Judicial Council of California, *Judicial Council of California Criminal Jury Instructions* (New York: Matthew Bender, 2021), CALCRIM No. 403, https://www.courts.ca.gov /partners/documents/calcrim-2021.pdf.

Session 3: Jesus, the Copycat Savior?

1. Lewis to Arthur Graves, October 18, 1931, in *The Collected Letters of C. S. Lewis*, ed. Walter Hooper, vol. 1, *Family Letters 1905–1931* (San Francisco: Harper, 2004), 977.
2. Lexico, s.v. "myth," accessed June 27, 2020, https://www.lexico.com/en/definition/myth.

Session 3: Secondary Investigation

1. Charles Haddon Spurgeon, *The Saint and His Saviour: The Progress of the Soul in the Knowledge of Jesus* (London: Hodder & Stoughton, 2006), 16.
2. *Merriam-Webster*, s.v. "idolatry," accessed April 5, 2021, https://www.merriam-webster .com/dictionary/idolatry.
3. Preston Greene, "Are We Living in a Computer Simulation? Let's Not Find Out," *New York Times*, August 10, 2019, https://www.nytimes.com/2019/08/10/opinion/sunday/are -we-living-in-a-computer-simulation-lets-not-find-out.html.
4. Greene, "Are We Living in a Computer Simulation?"

Session 4: Jesus, the Mistaken Messiah?

1. Judicial Council of California, *Judicial Council of California Criminal Jury Instructions* (New York: Matthew Bender, 2021), CALCRIM No. 336, https://www.courts.ca.gov /partners/documents/calcrim-2021.pdf.

2. *Judicial Council of California Criminal Jury Instructions*, CALCRIM No. 336.
3. From Peter Stoner's 1958 book *Science Speaks* as cited in Josh McDowell, *More Than a Carpenter* (Wheaton, IL: Living Books, 1977), 107.

Session 5: Secondary Investigation

1. George Whitefield, "Christ, the Support of the Tempted," *Sermons of George Whitefield* (Peabody, MA: Hendrickson, 2009), 68.
2. Gail Godwin, *Dream Children: Stories* (New York: Ballantine, 1996), 102.

Session 6: Secondary Investigation

1. Géza Vermes, *The Changing Faces of Jesus* (New York: Penguin, 2002), 8.
2. Judicial Council of California, *Judicial Council of California Criminal Jury Instructions* (New York: Matthew Bender, 2021), CALCRIM No. 105, https://www.courts.ca.gov /partners/documents/calcrim-2021.pdf.

Session 7: Jesus, the Dreary Deity?

1. For more on the basilica at Ottobeuren Abbey, refer to Wikipedia, s.v. "Ottobeuren Abbey," last modified January 23, 2021, https://en.wikipedia.org/wiki/Ottobeuren _Abbey; or "Ottobeuren Abbey," Bavaria, accessed September 7, 2020, https://www .bavaria.by/experiences/city-country-culture/churches-monasteries/ottobeuren-abbey/.

Session 7: Secondary Investigation

1. Martin Luther, "Preface to Georg Rhau's Symphoniae Iucundae, 1538," *Liturgy and Hymns* (Minneapolis: Fortress, 1965), 321.

Session 8: Secondary Investigation

1. Maria Montessori, *The Absorbent Mind: A Classic in Education and Child Development for Educators and Parents* (New York: Holt, 1995), 283.
2. John Calvin in Lars P. Qualben, *A History of the Christian Church* (Eugene, OR: Wipf & Stock, 2008), 270.

Session 9: Jesus, the Science Denier?

1. Annie Laurie Gaylor, "Catherine Fahringer," Freedom from Religion Foundation, accessed September 28, 2020, https://ffrf.org/news/day/dayitems/item/14551-catherine -fahringer.

Session 9: Secondary Investigation

1. V. J. McBrierty, *Ernest Thomas Sinton Walton, The Irish Scientist, 1903–1995* (Dublin: Trinity College Dublin Press, 2003), 58.
2. Refer to Lee Rainie, Scott Keeter, and Andrew Perrin, "Trust and Distrust in America," Pew Research Center, July 22, 2019, https://www.pewresearch.org/politics/2019/07/22 /trust-and-distrust-in-america/.
3. New World Encyclopedia, s.v. "Johannes Kepler," accessed September 25, 2020, https:// www.newworldencyclopedia.org/entry/Johannes_Kepler.